Tamil Female Civil Space

Its Evolution and Decline in Tamil Eelam

N. Malathy

AAKAR

Tamil Female Civil Space

N. Malathy

First Published 2019

ISBN 978-93-5002-622-9

Cover Image: From the January 1994 issue of *Suthanthira Paravaikal* depicting an Eelam Tamil female idol Ariyaaththai who one hundred years ago tamed a rogue elephant and was killed for the same.

Published by
AAKAR BOOKS
28 E Pocket IV, Mayur Vihar Phase I
Delhi 110 091 India
aakarbooks@gmail.com

Laser Typeset at
Arpit Printographers, Delhi

Printed at
D.K. Fine Art Press, Delhi

Contents

Abbreviations

CWR - Centre for Women Research
CWDR - Centre for Women Development and Rehabilitation
ENLF - Eelam National Liberation Front
EPRLF - Eelam People's Revolutionary Liberation Front
EROS - Eelam Revolutionary Organization of Students
LTTE - Liberation Tigers of Tamil Eelam
PLOTE - People's Liberation Organization for Tamil Eelam
SOLT - Student Organization of Liberation Tigers
SP - Suthanthira Paravaikal (Freedom Birds)
TELO - Tamil Eelam Liberation Organization
TLO - Tamil Liberation Organization
TSU - Tamil Students Union
TYU - Tamil Youth Union
WRC–Women Research Centre

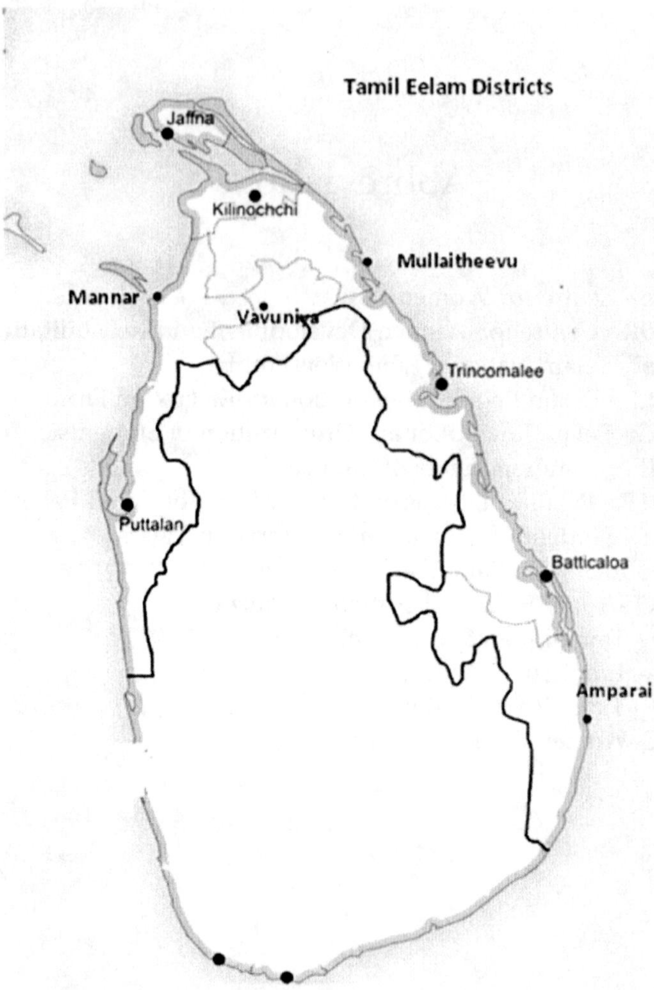
Tamil Eelam Districts
Jaffna
Kilinochchi
Mullaitheevu
Mannar
Vavuniya
Trincomalee
Puttalan
Batticaloa
Amparai

Place Names Appearing in the Map

Jaffna is the most heavily populated district in **Tamil Eelam**.

Vadamaradchi is the northern part of Jaffna peninsula.

VVT (Pirapaharan's birthplace) and Nelliyadi are in Vadamaradchi

Thenmaradchi is the southern part of Jaffna peninsula.

Chavakachcheri and Kilali near it are in Thenmaradchi.

Valigaamam is the western part of Jaffna peninsula.

Kalviyankaadu, Mallakam, Chunnakan, Suthumalai, Kokkuvil, Kondavil, Kopay, Palali, Karainagar, Sanganai and Nichchaamam are some place names in this region mentioned in the book.

Vanni refers to the combined region that includes the four districts:

Vavuniya includes Palamoddai

Mannar includes Adampan and Silavathurai

Kilinochchi was the LTTE de facto state's capital.

Mullaitheevu was where the LTTE had most of its military centres. The following place names mentioned are in this district: Manalaaru, Puthukkkudiyiruppu, Alampil, Visuvamadu, Kumulamunai, Mankulam, Vadduvahal, and Kepapulavu.

Batticaloa includes Arayampathi

Trincomalee includes Pattalipuram and Moothoor.

Preface

Revolutions aim to eliminate oppression. They are cyclic and are part of human existence. In Tamil Eelam there was a revolution taking place. The revolutionaries in this scene were not given the time to continue this cycle because this revolution was abruptly brought to a halt through a genocide. In this revolution, Eelam Tamil women who were very much kept in the private space by their society, briefly burst into the public space from the early 1980s till 2009. This book is a documentation of that history as told by the women themselves. This phase of women bursting into the public space has now been lost. Thus it is even more urgent to record it.

The majority of Eelam Tamil women and even other women of South Asia are unable to imagine a social fabric where they are not oppressed. The process of de-oppression is a long path and the women have a long way to go. Thus they are unable to even imagine this liberating social ethos. The Eelam Tamil women went a long way along this path during that short period of about 25 years. It is not easy to convey, through a history project such as this, that revolutionary social fabric they managed to create. That is, however, a motivation for this project. The reader must judge the success or failure of this goal. This goal aside, the book is also a documentation of the history of that rapture.

Like most histories of the people at the margins of the current global order, Eelam Tamil history has been written mostly by 'others'. If one looks somewhat deeper, these 'others' have all been either influenced or motivated by the dominant global order. This global order has been against the struggle of Eelam Tamils ever since the time of Western colonialism, especially the British colonialism. Therefore, the history of the Eelam Tamil struggle written by these writers invariably has overt or subtle positions against Eelam Tamil self-determination. The geopolitical aspect of the Eelam Tamil struggle has become increasingly apparent through the conduct of the United Nations (UN), India and the UK-USA axis after 2009. This book is not about the geopolitical dimension of the Eelam Tamil struggle. Yet, in order to give the reader a glimpse of this evolving geopolitical dimension, as the history of the women's rapture evolved, short texts are provided at the end of some chapters that will elucidate this.

Women's violence and violence against women are today popular topics of investigation by the UN, the academia and the journalists. Since the UN declaration of the 'Convention on the Elimination of All Forms of Discrimination Against Women' in 1979 there is a noticeable growth of 'women's violence' on the ground. In many theatres of conflict women have not only been the victims of violence but have also become armed combatants. According to the experts they are 'perpetrators of violence'. To this date women's violence has been mainly in battles against a better armed enemy who is oppressing their community. Given this a more empathetic treatment of women's violence by the 'experts' seems a rational approach. Yet, reality is the opposite. The second form of violence that is violence on women is extensively reported as needing the attention of the world, while the first, that is women's violence as part of armed struggles, is portrayed negatively. As a result most of the writing on this topic tends to be a 'specialist branch' of the 'counter insurgency' literature.

Women have partaken in large numbers in various armed struggles for about 40-50 years. Invariably women have joined these armed struggles a few years after the armed group had been formed and the struggle had been waged by the men.

Women's emancipation is often promoted by such groups. One reason, of course, is to increase female recruits which the 'experts' emphasize as the main reason.

As already stated, the main subject matter of this work is about Eelam Tamil women bursting into the public social space during the armed struggle for Tamil Eelam independence. Almost all the writing on this specific subject is about the women in the Liberation Tigers of Tamil Eelam (LTTE). These writings were mainly written by those influenced by the dominant global view on armed struggles and women's participation in it. Thus these writings are blind to the positive aspect and focused mainly on the negative side of this phenomenon. There are two exceptions but even these two focus only on the growth of the battle capabilities of the women in this group.[1,2] This current effort is different. It focuses mainly on the societal changes caused by this phenomenon. Bringing out this otherwise ignored experiential history is not only useful knowledge it can also give lessons for future struggles of any people.

History correctly understood is only perceptions formed by viewing small parts of a vast human endeavour. Writing the histories of armed struggles is further compounded by the secrecy such struggles necessitate and the deep wounds, both physical and mental that the participants of the struggle end up carrying within them. In the case of the armed struggle of Tamil Eelam, the secrecy is necessary on two fronts. The existing global atmosphere continues to threaten participants of the struggle as war criminals instilling fear of speaking out. The rigid reverence for the struggle created by the sacrifices of their comrades also prevents them from talking about the history objectively.

The information for this project was sourced from the author's personal experience of living among the women for several years[3], written history by the women themselves which is described in Chapter 10 and women informers who talked post-2009. In addition to the writings of Tamil women, that of Adele Balasingam on the history of women's involvement must also be noted here.

A number of the pioneer women who were part of one or the other of the Eelam Tamil armed groups had either migrated or received asylum in another country. This migration accelerated after the Black July pogrom of 1983 and continued throughout the 1980's and the 1990's. The reasons for the pioneer LTTE women to leave the areas of Tamil Eelam that was under the LTTE administration are also many. Some were sent away by the LTTE, for treatment of battle injury, to either Tamil Nadu or to the West. Others had wanted a reprieve from their long service to the armed struggle. These women who had begun life in another country before 2009 are one category of useful informers. Having found a safe zone and reasonably settled, they are the ones in the best position in the current climate to be informers of a history project. This category of potential informers is mainly living in Tamil Nadu or in a Western country.

Another group of pioneer women had either found asylum or are in the process of seeking asylum in another country after being subjected to the genocidal assault in 2009. These women are not in a safe zone even after they have obtained asylum. Their safety, economy, physical health and mental well-being have all been very severely compromised. This is the second category of valuable informers.

The third category are those still left in Tamil Eelam and are living under extreme fear of torture, sexual assault, arrest or extrajudicial killing.

Informers to this history project have come from all three categories of women. Some potential informers from all three categories flatly refused to talk about their roles. Some cited mental trauma, while others cited objection from their respective families. Many exhibited a readiness-avoidance approach. These women when in conversation showed willingness to share their experiences, but mostly resisted attempts to make subsequent contact. It was very puzzling and frustrating. Given their precarious situation it was unkind to forcefully chase after those who were reluctant to make subsequent contact. A desire and a heavy burden of responsibility to complete the task was a persistent push factor to pursue the women informers. At the same time great empathy for these women was a pull factor.

The women's readiness-avoidance behaviour is worth exploring further. The first thing to remember is that the vast majority of the pioneer LTTE women are presently young mothers with dependent children and they have lost their husbands. They, especially those in the second and third category, are in a dire economic situation. Having lost their revolutionary group and forced to return to the patriarchal Tamil society, very often these women are barred from speaking for any history project by their families—husbands, in-laws, and even children. Forced to become dependent women once again, they suffer family oppression once again.

When a woman in any one of the three categories prepares herself to share their experience, they have to then face the oppressive global environment. What is the global context today for a long-term member of the LTTE writing his or her history? All long-term members are today treated as potential war criminals. The global context continues to brand LTTE as a terrorist group. This pattern of conduct of the global establishment has been that whenever they are unable to avoid blaming the Lankan side for its atrocity, they try hard to drag the LTTE also as equally culpable. For this reason, it is on the lookout for potential candidates among the long-term ex-LTTE members on whom the charge of war crimes can be slapped. Whenever they fail to find any other crime which they can slap on the long-term members, they revert to their faked 'child recruitment' accusation.

An additional reluctance of the LTTE members stems from their own personal frustrations with the LTTE movement. Many shy away from airing this publicly because of the deep emotional connection they have for the LTTE-led struggle.

It must indeed be a very strong woman who can overcome all these barriers and be an informer in a history project that challenges the global position. The readiness-avoidance behaviour of the women is a reflection of the inner pride they have for their struggle and their inability to situate it in the global context in which they find themselves.

For this reason names of women informers, who are living today, have been changed except when stating some known facts. The informers mentioned in this project are: Mahes, Rani, Nila, Kamala, Kavitha, Lalitha, Kalai, Aruna and Santha from the pre-1990 group, Pavana, Kumi, Malar and Meena from the pre-1995 group. Besides these informers, information was obtained from dozens of other women, who are not named.

In a way, it is only in Tamil Nadu today that these women find the environment of support to situate themselves without alienation. Despite the environment of support in Tamil Nadu, these women live in constant fear of harassment by the Indian authorities if they take part in anything related to the Tamil Eelam struggle. More will be said about the environment faced by the women in the last chapter.

The book starts with a brief outline of the position of women in Tamil culture from antiquity till the time when the British colonials left the island. The issue of Tamil self-determination that was already brewing boiled over soon after leading to the launch of many armed groups seeking Tamil Eelam. This period of the evolution of the armed groups was very much a male phenomenon. There was occasional female participation during this phase which was a precursor to what was to come. The early 80s was the time when the energies of the women stirred in multiple spheres. This phase is covered in Chapters 3 and 4. The Indian military intervention that followed propelled women to very intense involvement in the armed struggle which also helped to induce greater levels of confidence among them. The departure of the Indian military and the socio-political space that became available was a time of experimentation by the women that lasted for five years. The mass exodus from Jaffna in 1995 and rebuilding the infrastructure in Vanni created a new experimental phase. This was again followed by the Norwegian brokered ceasefire phase. These different phases are roughly explored in separate chapters through the women's narratives.

For the majority of women, facing the post-2009 environment is like being transported to a very different and hostile world. Adjusting to this is traumatic. In order to complement their narratives, some excerpts from the writings of the women during the earlier phase are provided in Chapter 10. It may happen that a fear free atmosphere for Eelam Tamils will arise some time in the future. At that time more women will be willing to narrate their experiences which will enrich this narrative history.

This work was launched with the hope of capturing the Tamil women's revolution. Though this necessitates taking a historical approach, the readers are urged to read it as the documentation of a social evolution rather than a historical record.

I am grateful to Phil Miller, Bashana Abeywardena and others who gave evidence at the 2013 Permanent People's Tribunal hearing on the genocide complicity of the UK and the USA Their evidence educated me on the geopolitical dimension of the Tamil Eelam struggle. Thanks are also due to many male and female ex-members of the LTTE, who read the manuscript and made useful comments.

More importantly, how does one acknowledge those who made this work possible? The women, who contributed to this work, have given their lives, limbs, children, husbands and much more. Does it make sense to acknowledge them with words? I can only acknowledge them with tears.

June 2018 **N. Malathy**
New Zealand

1

Women in the Tamil World: Antiquity–1947 (The Past)

According to our current knowledge, life forms exist only on this earth. These life forms began on the earth billions of years ago. As the life forms evolved the earth's crust shifted to form the continents that we know today. The evolution continued and resulted in modern-day humans 200,000 to 250,000 years ago in Africa. The humans eventually spread across the entire globe and lived as hunter-gatherers using tools made of stones, bones and antlers for nearly 200,000 years.

About 15,000 years ago, they painted on cave walls, built shelters, made sculptures with stones and bones and developed language for communication. Approximately 10,000 years ago the last ice age that covered the earth had ended and as the ice melted away larger animals like mammoth and saber tooth tigers became extinct paving the way for smaller animals and new kinds of plants. Increased human population necessitated farming in permanent agricultural settlements and domesticating animals. Humans also started to use copper and iron tools. As we fast forward to 8,000 years ago, farming villages begin to appear in the fertile areas of the globe. This in turn led to further population growth. Early cities appeared in Mesopotamia, Egypt and the Indus Valley. Written language appeared in these cities, 4,000 years ago. Thus began the great stories of civilizations. Empires rose and fell over the globe. All big empires and even smaller societies adopted religions to keep the people pacified.

In this vastness of humanity are a people, occupying the southern land mass of the Indian subcontinent, which 10,000 year ago also included the island of Sri Lanka. Even today tiny islands in the narrow strait between the two land masses makes it possible to view this strait as connecting rather than separating. Over a two thousand-year period the people in this region owing to various historical processes evolved into different language groups, Tamil, Telugu, Kannada, Malayalam and Sinhala. Till the intervention of Western colonialism these two land masses, southern parts of the Indian subcontinent and the island of Sri Lanka existed as a unified economic and cultural unit.

The history of Tamils of this region is extracted through its 2,000-year-old literature which is the oldest among the different languages mentioned above. Archaeology has also contributed to the writing of this history of Tamils. The discovery of the 'Keeladi' archaeological site in Tamil Nadu in 2013 is considered a major milestone in learning the history of Tamils. The Tamil region of India boasts of more than 50 per cent of the inscriptions to be found throughout the subcontinent. This together with the rich collection of literature indicates a highly literate Tamil society. Oldest literature in Tamil is all about nature, love and war, considered the oldest secular literature in the world. These are dated from 300 BC-200 BC.

Much earlier than this period of secular literature among Tamils, in the northern parts of the Indian subcontinent, ritualistic religious writings based on the caste theory were being written in Sanskrit. Religious teachers opposing this ritualistic caste-based teachings arose around 400 BC. This included the teachings of Buddhism and Jainism. These two religions which promoted an ascetic life to serve the people swept across the subcontinent because they appealed to ordinary people. One such religion that evolved in the Tamil land is the religion of Samanam. Mainstream scholarship equates this with Jainism though there are Tamil scholars who assert that Samanam is indigenous to Tamils. Whatever that may be, around 200 CE, the texture of Tamil literature changes from secular works to moral teachings and epics of common people with religious leanings. The literature from this period onwards till 700 CE was mostly written by Samanar and includes some of the most celebrated literature in Tamil, Tholkaappiyam, Thirukkural, Silappathikaaram and Manimeekalai. Despite the rich intellectual output of this period, for reasons described in the following paragraphs, Tamil historians referred to this period as the 'Dark Ages'.

Division of labour based on hereditary trade must have existed in the Tamil society over this period though it is not very evident in the literature of the period. Indeed religions, such as Buddhism, Jainism, and Samanam, which rose in opposition to the caste theory of the Sanskrit tradition, that also produced the impressive worldly literature that propagated equality of everyone.

Charting the evolution of women's position in the society since early times is also possible through the study of old Tamil literature. The 2,000-year-old, oldest secular Tamil literature, is a collection of poetry called the Sangam poetry. It consists of the works of about four hundred poets of whom about forty are considered to be women. Of them one name Ovaiyaar continues to be an icon even today, though her work is not commonly known to the Tamils of today. The society of this period was agricultural and women appear to have had a life outside their homes.

The period following the Sangam period is the period of epics. The two most prominent Tamil epics, Silappathikaaram and Manimeekalai were written during this period. These two epics have several women as the lead characters, attesting to a continuation of the position of women in the public space. Of all the female characters in these epics, Kannagi claims a lasting place in the Tamil mind as an icon of female power in the face of injustice. Indeed there are temples for her throughout the Tamil region.

A different kind of literature, devotional literature, commonly referred to as Bhakti[4] literature, began dominating the Tamil land from 700 CE onwards. This period also coincided with the foreign rule of Pallavar[5]. From this period onwards, Tamils wrote nothing but Bhakti literature and lost the worldly intellectual leanings of their ancestors. One foreign scholar even wondered if Tamils had lost their worldly intellectual culture forever.

The Bhakti tradition in Tamil lands was temple centred and cities grew around large temples endowed with vast land. Some writers have claimed that people who worked in these temple lands were permanently bonded to this work. Much of the celebrated architecture of Tamil Nadu such as the Mahabalipuram rock carvings and the massive Tanjavoor temple are a product of Pallavar and Chola[6] empires that promoted the Bhakti tradition. Temples that arose as part and parcel of the Bhakti tradition were dominated by the elites of the society. The lower caste people in all the Tamil land tended to have local temples for local deities. These too gradually fused with the dominant Bhakti tradition, entrenching caste in society.

Proponents of the Bhakti tradition claim that it rose in opposition to the caste theory. Those who advanced this view say that the religious teachers of the Bhakti tradition came from all castes. If that is so, it is clear that the Bhakti tradition had failed to remove caste practices. In reality, the Bhakti phase of Tamil history, lasting more than one thousand years, also intensified the caste practices propagated by the Sanskrit scriptures. The rise of the Bhakti tradition also coincided with the fall of those religions, Jainism, Buddhism and Samanam, that rose in opposition to caste theory.

As the Bhakti period emerges, women also appear to lose some ground in the Tamil literature of this period which was entirely based on Bhakti. During the more than one thousand years of Bhakti literature only three female poets are mentioned: Karaikal Ammaiyaar (CE 5th century),

Aandaal (CE 7th century) and Avudai Akka (CE 18th century). Of these three women two of them emerged during the very early centuries of the Bhakti period. It is also worth noting that these two women were among the very first of the Bhakti tradition poets, emerging closer to the earlier period. A second Ovaiyaar also appeared later in the 12th century and sang poems of the code of conduct. Tamils of today are more likely remember to her works rather than the works of the Ovaiyaar of the earlier Sangam period.

During this Bhakti period, the earlier epic period is referred to as the 'Dark Ages'. The Bhakti period continued for more than one thousand years when women continuously lost ground in the public space. The Bhakti movement dominated the Tamil mind when the Western colonialists began ruling the South Asian region. It is only in the recent decades, after the colonialists left the land, that the Tamils began to think about things other than Bhakti. Tamils are yet to write the kind of masterpieces they were able to create prior to the Bhakti phase that began in 700 CE. Ironically Tamil historians even today refer to the golden period of Tamil literature written mostly by Samanar as the 'Dark Ages' because the Tamil mind is even today consumed by the Bhakti religion. This trend began to be disturbed only with the struggle for independence from Western colonialism in the middle of the 20th century.

The Marina beach in Chennai hosts statues of many iconic Tamil historical figures. Among them only two are statutes of historical women, namely, Kannagi of Silappathikaaram of the post-Sangam period and the second Ovaiyaar of the Bhakti period. It would be wrong to imply that these two women though active in the public space were free of male dominance. The Kannagi story at one level depicts her dedication to her husband and the second Ovaiyaar also promoted the wife's subordination to her husband.

This relatively known history of Tamils in southern India evolved parallel to and together with the history of Eelam Tamils in the island. The Eelam Tamil connection, besides the geographic connection between southern India and the island, has been recently discovered and include inscriptions in the Tamil Brahmi[7] script in the island that predates the arrival of Buddhism. The rest of the history of this region is the changing fortunes of kings, big and small and the growth of Tamil-speaking and Sinhala-speaking people in separate parts of the island. It must also be noted that a more in-depth archaeological research on Tamil history in the island is hampered by the Sinhala Buddhist nationalist governments that have ruled the island since the departure of the British colonials.

The southern regions of the subcontinent including the island had a sea trading relationship with the ancient Arab, Greek and Roman empires. Unlike in northern parts of the subcontinent where Islam was spread through war and conquest, in the southern parts including the island, Arab trade contributed to the spread of Islam. Those converted to Islam are now called Muslims and it so happens that all the Muslim people in the island spoke Tamil rather than Sinhala.

Colonial Period: 1630-1947

The island, including the Tamil region, had trade connections with the Western empires of Greece and Rome as well as with the Arab empires long before the Western colonials arrived around the 16th century. When the Western colonials began arriving, the region was ruled by native kings, big and small. In the island, three such kingdoms have been established: Kotte kingdom, which includes the present-day Colombo; the Kandy kingdom and Jaffna kingdom that spanned the Tamil Eelam region.

The first Western colonials to arrive were the Portuguese at the beginning of the 16th century. Their advances were resisted by all the three kings and the chieftains of the three kingdoms. The last king of the Jaffna kingdom, Sangilian, is remembered for his bravery in resisting the Portuguese. The Portuguese managed to capture the Kotte and Jaffna kingdoms but failed to capture the Kandy kingdom due to its geography. The Portuguese were displaced by the Dutch colonials and then by the British. The Tamil resistance continued throughout the 500 years of colonial rule. One Vanni chieftain, Pandaravanniyan, who bravely fought to expel the British, from his Vanni kingdom, is another celebrated hero of the Tamils. The British eventually managed to gain control of the Kandy kingdom as well. In the 19th century, the British brought a unitary governing system to the island. Throughout the colonial occupation and also during the constitution making process in the last decades of British rule, Eelam Tamils resisted the unitary governing system and they continue to resist it to this day.

The British also promoted the new theory of the Aryan race of the Europeans. The British included the Sinhala people as part of this Aryan race, based on the mythology of the origin of Sinhala people, described in the Sinhala Buddhist chronicle *Mahavamsa*. Perhaps due to this, the struggle for independence from the colonial rule was not as passionate among the Sinhalese as it was in India. When compared to the spirit of struggle in India, even the spirit of struggle among the Eelam Tamils was greatly diminished, probably because of the fear of Sinhala majoritarian rule that would result after independence under the prevailing unitary governing system. While there are many notable Tamil women in Tamil Nadu who were active in the independence struggle, it is hard to find women of Tamil Eelam who had been active in this struggle. Thus it appears, at least in Tamil Eelam, the withdrawal of women from the public space, which started with the Bhakti movement one thousand years ago, had continued throughout the colonial times.

Geopolitics-1 (Till the End of the Colonial Period)

Human societies lived as hunter gatherer groups for more than 100,000 years. In other words for more than 95 per cent of their existence humans had lived as hunter gatherers. Cooperation and community feelings would have been the basis for organizing these communities. The sedentary life of humans began only about 10,000 years ago. Kings and queens, religion as a tool for keeping the people pacified, and social stratification begins here. The present phase of human social organization begins about 500 years ago with the European colonization. The last 100 years of post-colonial time, where government by people had been promoted as the organizing principle, had not matured to a level where it can be viewed as distinct from the colonial phase. But this process is ongoing. The geopolitical dimension of any problem of a people must be analysed from this perspective.

The geopolitical dimension of the Tamil struggle was not widely discussed in the media, not even in the Tamil owned media, until Taraki Sivaram[8] was interviewed by the International Human Rights Association[9] in 2004. The interview was also distributed by Tamilnet.com. Till then, India was the only external power, whose interest and involvement in the Eelam Tamil issue had been widely mentioned. In hindsight, one could see that even the Tamil owned media was subservient to the Western media which of course would never include the interests of the Western powers in its analysis. Post-2009, especially after the Permanent People's Tribunal (PPT)[10] held in Germany in 2013, one can observe some shifts, to include other foreign powers, in the analysis of the island's conflict. The evidence presented at the PPT, looked at the conflict from the colonial period onwards. The summary of that evidence is as follows.

The strategic importance of the island for trade and military purposes was recognized during the European colonial era which began more than 500 years ago. Prior to the British takeover of the island, other European powers, Portuguese,

Dutch and French, have also fought over the island. The Portuguese and Dutch colonists ruled parts of the island and their interest in the island was purely to use it as a port for the sea lanes in the Indian Ocean for trading purposes. Thus these colonials administered the different regions of the island as they found them. Britain, on the other hand, saw the island as a strategic military location to control India. Britain was exploiting the wealth and resources in India to fuel its own industrial and military growth. The Indians revolted against the British rule. Britain used the island as a safe base to control the restive India. There are documented comments by British officials as to why Britain can never give up control of the island as a military asset.

Britain faced a serious threat to this important military asset. Revolt of the Indian people against Britain was contagious to the Eelam Tamils in the island owing to their language and cultural links with Tamil Nadu in India. Britain adopted two strategies to manage this risk of the Eelam Tamils revolt against Britain, in the footsteps of the Indian people. First, Britain abolished the regional separation in the island that existed even during the earlier colonist times and made Sri Lanka into a unitary state giving total power to the majority community. Secondly, Britain created the theory that the Sinhala people are Aryans and are thus closer to the Europeans. It was a time when the Nazi ideology of superiority of Aryan people was predominant and it took the downtrodden Sinhala people by storm. The British colonists further substantiated the Sinhala Aryan theory by translating the Sinhala Buddhist chronicle *Mahavamsa* which till then was only available in Pali and thus unknown to the majority of the Sinhala people. The Sinhala people fully absorbed these theories which have propelled the anti-minority mindset of the Sinhala people that has been the source of the conflict in the island. These two strategies, the unitary government and the Aryan theory, effectively kept the island on Britain's side.

2

Women and the Tamil Eelam Struggle: 1947-1983

Most of the newly independent states, which gained independence during the 1950s and 60s after centuries of European colonialism, were in awe of the revolutions that had recently succeeded in the Soviet Union and China. Some form of socialism was on the lips of many citizens of the newly independent states and socialist political parties were popular. It is not surprising that the first stirrings of militant rebellion among the Eelam Tamils, known as the October 1967 revolution was led by the Communist Party of the island. It surfaced in societal location that was not directly connected to the Tamil Eelam armed struggle. The October 1967 revolt in Jaffna and the associated struggles for temple entry of those castes that were prevented from entering temples was an anti-caste rebellion. The left movement gave impetus to the anti-caste movement which would most certainly have existed ever since caste existed in South Asia. In Jaffna, where the worst forms of caste practices were followed in the island, the Communist Party of Ceylon took up the anti-caste struggle to its heights during the 1960s. The best known record of this anti-caste struggle is the book by Vehujanan[11]. An excerpt, from the book, reproduced in Appendix-A1, is educational for those who have no memory of this practice in Jaffna. Sadly, just three years later, the Tamil Eelam national struggle centred in Jaffna overtook this struggle. The effects of the earlier caste struggle on the armed movements that later evolved however was substantial. All the armed groups shunned caste and had the stated goal of creating a casteless society.

On the side of this anti-caste militancy there was no intended violence but the police and the oppressing high caste used violence against the militant protesters. Obscured in the documentation of this revolt are two incidents involving women. In one incident, the conviction and bravery of an older woman in the struggle is described[12]. In the incident an older woman had grabbed the gun from a policeman saying that the protesters would not be subdued by the threat of the gun. In the second incident a woman named Sellakili[13] was apparently on the search warrant of the police for throwing a grenade. She appears to be the first armed militant Eelam Tamil woman in contemporary times.

The British colonials left the island in 1947, giving it a unitary constitution. This brought the island under the Sinhala majoritarian rule. Eelam Tamil nationalism was visible even during the negotiations for the new constitution for the soon-to-be independent island but it was ignored by the colonials. Eelam Tamil nationalism soon crystalized as the Ilankai Tamil Arasu Katchi in 1949. The name implies a Tamil government for the Tamil people of the island. It was popularly known as the Federal Party in English because the party's policy was a federal system of government. It did not take long for the majoritarian rule to rear its ugly head with the Sinhala Only Language Act in 1956. This was quickly followed by the 1958 island wide pogrom against Tamils. During this phase the political struggle of Eelam Tamils took the form of mass protests lead by the Federal Party, which was the leading Tamil political party at that time. Eelam Tamils continued to face more than a decade of pogroms and marginalization in many spheres of life, including education, jobs, forced colonization, and land issues. These developments were priming the Eelam Tamil youth for armed struggle.

Thus, in the postcolonial era, the two most important layers in the Eelam Tamil social canvas are the struggles against extreme forms of the practice of 'caste untouchability' and the political struggle of unifying the fragmented social groups for self-rule. The participation of women in the mass protests of the political struggle also should be remembered to better comprehend what followed. The anti-caste struggle and the mass political protests had been instrumental in starting the process of bringing women into the public sphere.

While the general mood among Tamils against the Sri Lankan government had been building up, throughout the 1960s, the introduction of the 1970 university entrance scheme which required higher performance from areas with higher educational facilities was the initial impetus for the Tamil youth, in particular the Jaffna youth to seriously consider armed struggle. These youths were the worst affected by this scheme. They formed the Tamil Students' Union (TSU)[14] in 1970. The aim of this body was armed militancy. Young Tamil women, even though they too were affected by this university entrance scheme, did not have any active role in the group espousing militant politics. This is an indication of the conservative Jaffna society that promoted education and work for the young women but maintained strict societal codes that otherwise kept them restricted to their homes.

The TSU proved to be an important body only because many of the future male leaders of the various Tamil armed movements started their militant activities in this body. Most notable among them were Kuttimani and Pon Sivakumaran. According to some members of the TSU, Pirapaharan too, though was never a member of this body, had attended some of its meetings as a young boy. The activities of this student body included attempts to murder Tamil collaborators of the Sinhala regime. Its leaders and subsequently many of its members, including Sivakumaran, were arrested by the Sri Lankan armed forces. Many of them were later released. The arrests, however, resulted in the de facto end to this student body. Soon after Kuttimani, Pon Sivakumaran and Pirapaharan had all formed independent groups to carry out political violence. Of them Pon Sivakumaran acted without a formal group and in 1974 became the first militant to take his own life by biting the cyanide capsule to avoid being in police custody. Two young women who were friends of Pon Sivakumaran's sister, Valli and Atputham, had joined him as assistants to his militant acts. These two women appear to be the first Eelam Tamil women to participate in the Tamil Eelam armed struggle for independence. Thus as early as 1973 the spirit of armed militancy had begun the process of crossing the gender boundary in Tamil Eelam.

Parallel to Pon Sivakumaran or even slightly earlier, Kuttimani had also formed his own group and was involved in armed militancy. There are however no reports of women's participation in his group at this stage. Pirapaharan also formed the New Tamil Tigers around 1972. It too did not have female participation at this stage.

With the dissolution of the TSU which was formed in 1970, a new group of young men came together to form the Tamil Youth Union (TYU) in 1973 also with the intention of armed militancy. Pushparaja, a key player in this body, had published its history in his memoirs in 2006[15]. Uma Maheswaran who was to later lead one of the five main armed groups was active in the TYU but operated mostly from Colombo. The TYU had many female members. Notable were Urmila, Pushparaja's sister Pushparani, Kalyani and several others noted in Pushparaja's memoirs. Many in this group, including Pushparaja, were disillusioned that this group was coming under too much influence of the moderate leadership of the Tamil political party, TULF. TULF was a coalition of all Tamil parties which had been formed a few years earlier. They left the TULF to form the more militant Tamil Eelam Liberation Organization (TLO) in 1975. According to Pushparaja and also Pushparani who also published her own brief memoirs in 2012, women were active in the TLO, though there is no documentation suggesting that women in the TLO handled arms.

Sivakumaran's helpers Atputham and Valli, as well as Urmila, Pushparani, and several other women who were involved with the TLO, can be considered the pioneers of female participation in the Eelam Tamil armed militancy. Although none of them is known to have used arms themselves. Within two years of its formation the TLO itself was disbanded due to arrests or exile of its members.

Another notable group with armed struggle in mind that remained mainly a male outfit was the Eelam Revolutionary Organization of Students (EROS) that was launched in 1975 in London. It had strong membership from the eastern districts. The EROS took the Muslim issue as one of its main focus, more so than the other groups. In 1976, the EROS established links with the Palestinian Liberation Organization (PLO) and began planning to set up camps to train Eelam Tamils in military and guerrilla warfare. The EROS opened their training camps for the other militant groups including the LTTE. A number of Tamils, including many who would later form the core of the other Tamil militant groups, started their militant careers in these camps. The EROS never became as militarily active as the later groups such as the LTTE, largely because its leadership continued to be based in London. Partly as a result of this, differences arose in 1979 among the EROS cadres in the island. The result was that the student wing of the EROS split up from the EROS in 1980 to form a new organization called the EPRLF.

Kuttimani's group that had existed as early as 1969 took on the name TELO in 1979. Kuttimani was arrested by the Sri Lankan Navy in the sea in 1981, as he was returning from India by sea. He was killed during the island wide 1983 pogrom against Tamils, when 53 arrested Tamils in the Welikade prison were also killed by the Sinhala prisoners.

The early 1980s saw the solidification of Kuttimani's group as the Tamil Eelam Liberation Organization (TELO), the formation of the People's Liberation Organization of Tamil Eelam (PLOTE) due to split in the LTTE and the formation of the Eelam People's Revolutionary Liberation Front (EPRLF) due to split in the EROS. These are the five main armed groups that dominated the Tamil political scene during the 1980s.

During this phase, especially after the 1983 pogrom, young women began enlisting in all five groups in substantial numbers.

Geopolitics-2

After Britain left the administration of the island to the Sinhala people, in other words after independence in 1948, the struggle by the Tamils intensified leading to armed struggle. Britain's direct military involvement in the island also intensified. Britain gave extensive military assistance to Sri Lanka overtly and covertly during the 1970s and 80s.

The Sinhala mainstream has since attempted to design its history to support the theories propagated by Britain based on the Mahavamsa and Aryan race. This had necessitated either modifying or erasing new archaeological evidence that was unearthed.

As the British Empire receded and the USA empire grew in strength globally, the two joined hands to safeguard their military interests in the island. For many decades after independence, India remained fearful towards Britain and the USA. Owing to this fear, India sided with the Soviet Union during the cold war era. This tension was the reason that India helped the Tamil militants and provided them with training in India.

One of the issues that brought this competition between India and the UK-USA into the open was the Voice of America (VOA) tower that was built in the island. Taraki Sivaram in his famous 2004 interview said that India and the Soviet Union suspected that this VOA tower was emitting extreme low frequency waves to detect submarines in the Indian Ocean. The Indian alignment with the Soviet Union ended with Indira Gandhi, the late Prime Minister of India who was assassinated by Sikh militants.

3

Early Stirrings Among Women: 1984-1987

The growth of the armed groups began amidst a heightened level of awareness of Tamil political rights among the Tamil populace. One expression of this can be seen in the Eelam Tamil art forms of poetry, prose and theatre created during this period when armed struggle starts to take shape. Poetry and drama in particular were used to spread the theme of political struggle[16]. One woman commented that more than poetry and drama, guerrilla attacks reaches people faster and within a short period it encourages reflection among people. This is indeed the theory that evolved from the Cuban revolution that was promoted by Che Guevara.

Women who were of school age during this period remembered how the atmosphere, even at home, was charged with the spirit of struggle. During this early stage, Tamil civilians did not differentiate between the armed groups and all the groups were admired and provided with food and safe houses. It is in this atmosphere, the women's enlistment in the armed movements starts to take shape. This early attraction for armed struggle among women was soon followed with women's activism against the war. This chapter will trace these early stirrings under three broad categories: enlistment of women in the four main armed groups that is the four except the LTTE, the women who protested against the violence and war, and the women who enlisted in the LTTE.

In 1984, as the women's role in the armed groups

increased, the EROS coordinated a united front for the EROS, the TELO and the EPRLF. This front was called the ENLF. The LTTE joined the ENLF a few months later. Efforts were made to bring in the PLOTE but were not successful. The PLOTE, however, remained close to the TULF, the moderate political party. The ENLF in coordination carried out attacks against government positions in Jaffna. The combined assaults led to the near-total disappearance of government authority in Jaffna. This unity remained only for less than two years. In 1986, the LTTE pulled out of ENLF. Two months later clashes erupted between the LTTE and the TELO. The TELO cadres, whether armed or unarmed, came under rifle attack and were shot dead. On May 5, the TELO's leader Sri Sabaratnam was shot dead. Over four hundred TELO cadres had been killed, and the TELO had been virtually wiped out. The LTTE justified its actions saying that the TELO was being used by India to infiltrate the Tamil Eelam struggle and reshape it to its own ends. Several years later, however, in 1990, Kittu, who had directed and led the attacks, admitted that it had been a mistake to kill the cadres of the TELO, although he justified the assassination of the top leaders. Later in 1986, LTTE attacked the EPRLF, inflicting heavy losses. Many of its cadres were killed or taken prisoner and its camps and weapons were seized by the LTTE.

The history of armed struggles are always formed and dominated by young males. That was also the case with the Eelam Tamils. Their history as in any history of armed struggle is also replete with cycles of forming a new armed group, splintering of existing groups, annihilation of one group by another; and sometimes merging of one or more groups. The subject of the history of armed movements in Tamil Eelam: their formative period during the 1970s, the elimination or absorption of all other armed groups by the LTTE in the mid-1980s; the disgruntled from the other groups as well as the LTTE, that is those who escaped being killed, finding sanctuary and space for activism around the world;

and the final history of the LTTE itself has not been studied in totality. While studies on the LTTE have been widespread, an all-encompassing study of Tamil armed movements is absent to date.

As is universally the case, the courage to get directly involved in the armed struggle does not pervade the society uniformly. To either take up arms or provide safe houses to hide the arms and the pooraalis[17] require a greater degree of courage and dedication. In Jaffna the families who offered their homes to the armed movements came to be called the 'source houses'. These are homes of families who provided support to the militants and can thus be trusted to help them when needed. It is worth noting that most of the early militant women, especially from Jaffna, came from these families. In these houses the young women came into direct contact with the male members of the armed movements and were exposed to their activities.

Enlistment of Women in the Other Four Armed Groups

From around 1983, the four major groups, that is all except the LTTE, had begun to actively attract women into their fold. They were mainly assigned to work in the community to raise political awareness on the Tamil issue. This awareness building work also included women's empowerment as well as other social issues like the caste divisions. Publications were produced and distributed. Community-based groups on women, fisherfolk, and other interest groups were established to discuss and address their issues. The 1983 state-sponsored pogrom against Tamils brought women in even larger numbers into these four armed groups. The contribution of these women in the four major groups in breaking the barriers for women to enter the public political space is substantial. Yet, despite some efforts by this author, written documents or women who could be informers of their history have been difficult to trace. One piece of information that is available is that the very first female maaveerar[18] in the Tamil Eelam armed struggle is a young woman named Shoba belonging to the EPRLF movement. She was killed in battle in February 1986 during an attack on the Karainagar Lankan Naval base. The absence of documentation of women in these four movements may be due to the shortened period of only three or four years when they could openly function. From 1986, clashes began between the LTTE and the TELO and later on between the LTTE and the EPRLF. Both groups' resources were destroyed. The PLOTE movement also saw a gradual decline. The EROS was partially absorbed into the LTTE.

All the armed groups had also set up student bodies to create a network among the senior school students. Similarly another body was created among university students. Both these groups were also additional avenues for the women to enlist with these armed groups.

Young women, more so than young men, would join an armed group without their parents' knowledge. At the start these young women were not specific about which group they joined. However, as the different groups started to be critical of each other, the women too took sides with the group that was closest to them. Later women also joined by choosing a particular group.

Please note that this is one of the four areas marked in grey in the canvas-chart at the end of this chapter that ideally should be part of this study but has not been successful in documenting.

Enlistment in the LTTE

Unlike the other armed groups, the LTTE dragged its feet in enlisting women even after the 1983 pogrom when women expressed eagerness to take up arms. Thileepan, the Jaffna LTTE commander, however, realizing the importance of getting women involved, began attracting young women into the politico-social space.

Initially the Jaffna young women began training as first-aid helpers through the St Johns ambulance services in Jaffna.

It was difficult at the start because parents would not let their daughters go out in groups. In the end, it was really the Lankan military that helped to expand the network. Nila from Valigaamam recalled how when the military vehicles were brought in readiness for a move into the civilian space, people from the houses closest to the military camps would knock at the house next door to warn about the military's move. The warning of the potential military move through door knocking would be repeated till the entire area was forewarned. The young people, both men and women, would then leave the area. The LTTE would prepare places for them to stay. This also produced spaces for the young women to network. Even those parents, who objected earlier, agreed that for their own safety the young women had to leave home.

The young women soon gathered to get themselves trained in first aid and primary healthcare. Medical students were linked to give the training in different places. The women assembled more women for the training. After the training the young women opened first-aid centres all around Jaffna and provided free service to the people.

Another woman from the early days Rani, from Vadamaradchi, began working after school from the age of 14. She recalled the first aid training given in her area by Pathmalojani, who was a Sri Lankan trained medical doctor working in a hospital. Pathmalojani, later joined the LTTE and took on the name Elumathy. She continued to work as a doctor in the LTTE areas till the end of the war in 2009. She was among the thousands who were disappeared by the Lankan military at the end of the war. In those early days, Rani would come home from school and change into white hospital uniform and go for the first aid training given by Elumathy. By the time Rani was 17, she had given up school and had begun full-time work in the socio-politico space. She recalled:

> If I take the bicycle at 6 am, I will return home only at 8.30 pm. We started a primary healthcare-cum-first aid centre in

> each village. I was in charge of one. I recruited young women and made a roster to carry out the service. Vadamaradchi was targeted by the military with frequent shelling from different directions. A lot of people would be dying and no one would be willing to drive the victims to the hospital during such intense shelling. The young women as well as men would go into lanes or wherever shells had fallen and give treatment to the injured. We would treat serious head injuries, including scooping the brain back into the skull or the intestine back into the stomach. We would put victims in a cart and take them to medical people or others who would help. Long before these young women took military training, while wearing the traditional skirt and top, they had carried heavy first aid equipment to set up a first aid post just 100 metres behind the frontline to assist male pooraalis in battle.

In order to reach the women in the bottom strata of society, the women launched cottage industries in these first aid centres. Each first aid centre was to cater for two types of cottage industry. The produce from the cottage industry was exhibited in 1986 in a large exhibition that lasted a week. The produce was sold to the public. Women manned the stalls as well as cooked food to be sold. To implement this efficiently the young women had to stay away from home for that week. That was perhaps the first time families in Jaffna allowed their daughters to stay away from home for a project run by an armed group. It was a success and families now had the confidence to allow their daughters to stay away from home a few days at a time. Some parents even encouraged their daughters to get involved in this work. The cottage industry project brought women from all walks of life together creating comradeship among them. This also provided the women from the bottom strata with an independent income.

Around this time the schools were also not functioning regularly and the women implemented another project. Young women who were without work or schooling were selected and given pre-school teacher training. Pre-schools were begun with them as teachers. These teachers were expected to be more than just pre-school teachers. They also doubled up as social workers-cum-activists. They were to instruct the families on health, education and politics as well. These teachers were provided with the necessary training and seminars were held to prepare them for this task. Many older women also pitched in to help. These teachers and even their families had to be exemplars of the social changes that were sought. Though there were problems in this effort, positive changes were brought about by this pre-school approach. The pre-school movement, another one of Thileepan's brain child, became an important social movement for change.[19]

The young women also undertook specifically women's issues in families. They would visit the families in their allocated areas and befriend the women and gain their trust. This would lead to the women discussing their problems with the women activists. When serious issues came up, a trained counsellor was organized to meet the affected women to deal with her problems. Some of these women activists worked in the Muslim areas of Jaffna. These pioneer young women activists reported that the Muslim women were also very supportive and were gradually drawn into the activist circle. So much so that they even provided the LTTE pooraalis with food and food parcels through the young women activists. Sadly this positive relationship soured by 1990 to the extent that the entire Muslim population of around 100,000 were evicted from Jaffna by the LTTE.

Through all these social spaces such as: the St John's first aid service, the independent first aid and primary health care service, cottage industry efforts, pre-school movement, Kalvi Valarchi Kalaham and SOLT, young women formed strong networks. The radically minded among them, who had no public space opened to them to act previously, now began thinking of women's empowerment as part of the struggle. Some women in the Vadamaradchi region began gathering regularly to discuss various issues mainly related to women.

Initially these meetings were held under the supervision of the regional male poruppalar[20]. However, soon women held the meetings on their own. Women in other parts of Jaffna followed suit. The Vadamaradchi women's section published a book *Suthanthira Paravaikal* on women's issues in 1985. Following the publication of two issues of *Suthanthira Paravaikal* by the Vadamaradchi group, a special group was formed under the leadership of Aruna to publish regular issues. This publication was considered the official organ of the women's section of the LTTE. Though interrupted by war at various stages it continued publication for thirty years till 2008. Except for a few issues, most of the issues of the SP magazine appear to be lost, at least at the time of this writing[21].

As the young women's network expanded this name "Suthanthira Paravaikal" (SP) was adopted as the name of their organization. Once SP was formally established, it further expanded its network to cover all of Jaffna.

Nila, another SP activist from Valigaamam, recounted the role of Thileepan in the SP,

> Thileepan was a very good leader for us despite being a man. He urged all the women to be active and supported us all greatly. He was the main coordinator for the SP. He was the kind of leader who never reprimanded us but would always discuss alternative ways in which the task could have been handled.

Thileepan was assisted in coordinating the work of the SP by women put in charge for the three regions in Jaffna. Niththila and Santha were assigned the Vadamaradchi region. Thenmaradchi region was assigned to Lalitha and Rosani. Valigaamam being a larger region, more women were assigned to subdivisions within it. Among them were Aruna, Mithila, Nila, Helen, Kalai and Ahila.

While the SP gained popularity in the poorer areas of Jaffna, the SP was disparaged by the wealthy in Jaffna. They considered the SP women to be breaking traditions and roaming the streets at all hours. It was similar to the manner in which the women from the other armed groups were viewed. It must also be noted that the SP did not operate in affluent areas. Thus young women who lived in the rich areas remained oblivious to the work of other young women in Jaffna.

Another path available to the women to work with any of the armed groups was the student bodies created by these groups. Thileepan who coordinated the SP also had a role in the setting up of the Student Organization of the Liberation Tigers (SOLT). An educational assistance scheme called "Kalvi Valarchi Kalagam" had been launched by the LTTE to give after-school assistance to senior school students with their school work. This also provided a path for the senior students to join the LTTE student body SOLT.

Murali was in charge of this body which created the network among school students. A parallel student body Marumalarchi Kalagam was also set up in the Jaffna University. These two groups also drew young women into their fold. Unlike the women's groups like the SP, set up among the general population, these student bodies had greater prestige among the general Jaffna population. It is indicative of the reactionary social fabric of the Jaffna society that has its roots in the brutal caste system.

The SOLT activities were such that both genders could participate. Both girls and boys participated in equal numbers. SOLT had a set of written rules for participation in its activities. Some of its rules are: the members should obey the school rules and teachers' instructions—in other words, no activity should be in rebellion against the school; dress should be decent and neat; makeup such as nail polish or too many jewels should not be worn by the girls; and members should not get involved in love affairs. When joining SOLT, potential members had to sign a paper printed with these rules. Those whose behaviour was deemed to be not inline were side-lined. During this period of heightened awareness, SOLT became very popular. In most schools there was extensive participation.

SOLT members helped in collecting junk material for the manufacture of grenades. These were collected outside school hours and taken to the schools, from where, LTTE personnel came to collect them. Given the widespread injuries resulting from the ongoing war, first aid training was also given to all SOLT members. SOLT members also helped to care for the uprooted people who were being uprooted from their homes on a large scale. Stage productions were also produced about the inadequacies of the prevailing education and the importance of encouraging original thinking–a well-known drama along this line was called 'Palli Elunthiduveer' (wake up from slumber). SOLT members also went around giving instructions and assistance to civilians on digging bunkers for protection from aerial bombing. During temple festivals SOLT members manned bookshops selling struggle-related books.

Some of the women also talked about how young women were tested for their readiness for armed struggle by asking them to deliver food to pooraalis who were manning the sentry points. This was a task full of dangers. It brought the young women closer to the armed struggle they said.

Eventually women's role in the LTTE grew. Tamils often say that the LTTE's attraction to the Tamil mind can be attributed to two of its main features: successful military actions and strong discipline. Though LTTE too spoke of Marxism like the other Tamil armed groups, it did not spend its resources in awareness building in this regard. In fact the leader of LTTE had repeatedly maintained that one should not preach or boast but demonstrate by actions. To this end the LTTE ideology was to intake members, convert them into 'pooraali' with social/political awareness and make them fight for independence and liberation. All projects by the LTTE including its welfare projects had this also as its ulterior motive.

Entry of women into the public space provided many types of catalysts for social reconstruction. The practice of the caste system and the position of women in the society saw the most noticeable changes. The struggle provided different paths for the women to burst into the public sphere. These paths would have been hard to traverse without the atmosphere of intense struggle. The earlier anti-caste struggle was also quickly consumed by the armed struggle and the two merged into one. The changes to the practice of the caste system while closely intertwined with the changes to the position of women in the society followed an entirely different route. Some observations on this will be also be found in this study.

Neither the evolution of the five major armed groups nor the participation of women in them took place uniformly throughout the Tamil homeland. Indeed, detractors of the LTTE, which dominated the scene from 1986 onwards, had accused it of being overly focused on Northern-Jaffna. There are demographic, geographic, economic and environmental reasons for this Northern-Jaffna centrism. Even caste-based social rigidity was worst in Jaffna and the communist party led October 1967 revolution against untouchability was also centred in Jaffna. At the start of the armed struggle period, northern regions of Tamil Eelam in general and Jaffna in particular were unique in having a near 100 per cent Tamil-speaking population including the Muslims. The eastern regions on the other hand have a substantial Sinhala-speaking population worsened by the state-planned demographic changes since the 1950s. Based on the 1981 census, the following is the number of Tamils in the Tamil Eelam regions: Jaffna-700,000, Vanni-302,000, East-410,000. Thus the size of Tamil population in Jaffna is the same as the size in the rest of the Tamil homeland. These and other factors were behind Jaffna centrism on many matters pertaining to Tamil Eelam. It also impacted on the participation of women in the armed movements.

Ideally a study such as this should include and be based on narratives of women who participated in the armed struggle or were active against the armed struggle across the Tamil homeland. Unfortunately, Jaffna centrism is reflected in this study too. As will be seen in the following chapters this study is mainly about the LTTE women from the north but some efforts were made to include the other women who were active carrying arms or were active against the armed struggle. The picture marked canvas-chart is a two dimensional portrayal of relevant events for this study with time as x-axis and the geography as y-axis. The grey boxes show the topics that this study has failed to cover.

Carpentry

TV Repair

Bicycle Repair

Typewriter Repair

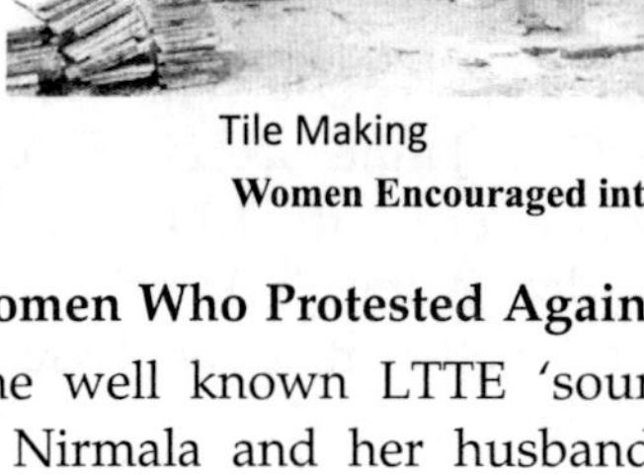

Tile Making

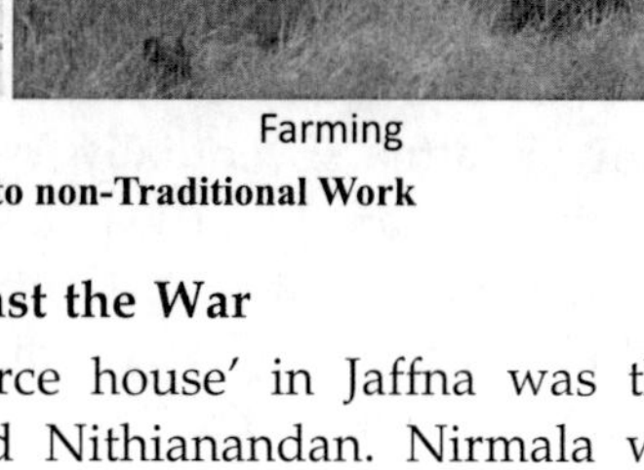

Farming

Women Encouraged into non-Traditional Work

Women Who Protested Against the War

One well known LTTE 'source house' in Jaffna was that of Nirmala and her husband Nithianandan. Nirmala was imprisoned by the Sri Lankan government for harbouring the LTTE. She was taken away from prison to India in a jail break carried out by the LTTE. She and her husband later fell out with the LTTE and she has since remained a critic of the LTTE, mainly accusing the LTTE of using women as cannon fodder. Rajini Thiranagama was Nirmala's sister and she was also drawn into the LTTE fold through Nirmala. Like Nirmala, Rajini too fell out with the LTTE for similar reasons.

During the mid-1980s the group, Women Research Circle (WRC), was set up inside the Jaffna University and Rajini Thiranagama, who was a lecturer in the medical college of Jaffna University, was the key person in this group. This group published a collection of poetry by Tamil women, *Sollaatha Seithikal*, and a translation of the work on feminism published in Colombo by a group called 'Feminist Study Circle'. WRC also setup the 'Poorani Illam' during the time of the Indian forces to support women made destitute by the war.

Rajini Thiranagama is also one of the four authors of the book, *Broken Palmyra*, published by the University Teachers for Human Rights (URHR), during the presence of the Indian forces for three years from 1987. It criticizes the Indian forces and the LTTE for their human rights violations. Rajini was assassinated in 1989 which her sister Nirmala and many others blame the LTTE. A university student Selvi, an activist and poet, also functioned in WRC and Poorani Illam. Selvi was arrested by the LTTE and had since gone missing suspected to have been executed by the LTTE. Following these events, a similar body, Surya Development Centre, with goals similar to Poorani Illam was launched in Colombo in 1990, to care for women from the rest of the island, made destitute by the war. It initially coordinated its work with the Poorani Illam in Jaffna. Eventually WRC in Jaffna became defunct and the Poorani Illam was taken over by the LTTE women and it evolved into the Centre for Women's Development of Rehabilitation (CWDR) that functioned as an NGO in areas under the LTTE. Surya Development Centre shifted to

Batticaloa and continues to operate today with funds from international donors, including USAID. It also brings out a regular publication that covers women's issues and is probably the only such publication on women's issues in Tamil in the Tamil homeland at present.

Note that this is another area of women's activism that this study has been unable to fully cover.

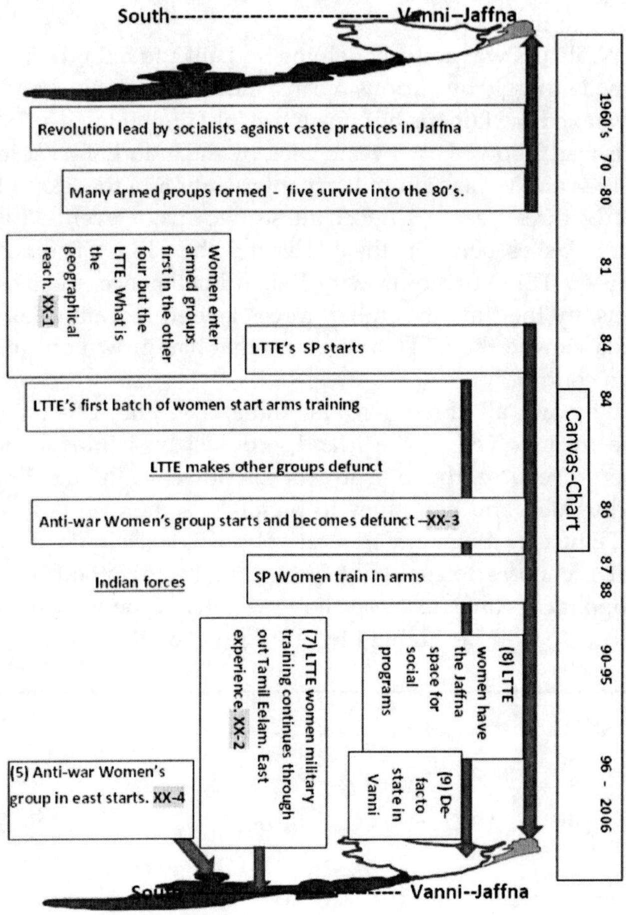

Geopolitics-3

After the assassination of the Indian Prime Minister, Indira Gandhi in 1984, her son Rajiv Gandhi, took over her position. His time as Prime Minister coincided with major changes in the world order with the dissolution of the Soviet Union and the rise of a single super power, the USA. Under Rajiv Gandhi, India opened its markets to globalization and moved closer to the UK-USA.

While UK was actively helping Sri Lanka to fight the Tamil armed struggle by various means, India under Rajiv Gandhi, organized the famous but unsuccessful Thimbu talks in 1985. This was followed, two years later, by the Indo-Lanka accord of 1987 and the Indian military intervention in the island for nearly three years. Between these two major events, there were clashes between the LTTE and the TELO. The LTTE accused TELO of siding with Indian intelligence, the RAW. Thus, by the time the Indian forces landed in Tamil Eelam, India viewed the LTTE as a group that had grown out of its own control.

By now, all three powers, India, UK and USA, were directly involved in the island's conflict by joining hands. Their discourse, the mainstream discourse on the LTTE has highlighted and continues to highlight some events in the LTTE history to portray it negatively. This selection of events that it chooses to highlight ought to be understood in this geopolitical context. These chosen events of the mainstream discourse will be highlighted in the geopolitics boxes that follow.

4

First Batch Training in Tamil Nadu: 1984-1985

As we saw in the last section, the women enlisted by the other groups and even those who joined the SP movement were seen in a derogatory light by the Jaffna public. They were not given respectful recognition for the work they were doing. For this reason, the section of the LTTE in Jaffna, under the LTTE leader Kittu, dragged its feet in enlisting women for arms training. However, seeing that women were enlisting in large numbers in the other groups, Pirapaharan and the Vanni section of the LTTE under Mathaya and Victor started a programme of enlisting young women from outside Jaffna to be sent to Tamil Nadu for arms training. Thus all the ninety women who trained in the first LTTE women's batch in 1984, except about nine among them, were from the Vanni districts.

One group of women from Jaffna in this batch consisted of four women, Mathy, Janani, Jeya and Vanaja. Mathy and Janani who were studying at the Peradeniya campus in Kandy were affected by the 1983 island-wide pogrom against Tamils. Refusing to attend the Peradeniya campus, they went on a protest fast in Jaffna demanding that they be transferred to study in the north. Jeya and Vanaja who were studying at Jaffna University joined the fast to support them. When their fasting continued and their lives were at risk, they were taken away to Tamil Nadu by the LTTE to break up their protest fasting. In Tamil Nadu, they were placed under the care of Anton and Adele Balasingam. One of these four women, Mathy, married Pirapaharan and did not take the training. The other three took the training in the first batch. Janani was later to head the Senchchoolai children's home and Jeya held the post of 'Head of women's political wing' for five years. Another group of six women, originating from Jaffna and Vanni, had joined the TELO and were sent by the TELO to Tamil Nadu. This group of six women broke away from the TELO and surrendered to the LTTE and were also placed under Adele's care. Among them was Sothiya who became the first leader of the women's military division. After her death, one of the two women's military regiments was named after her. Three more women had already arrived in Tamil Nadu either with their families or for the purpose of study. One woman from the TELO group, Mahes, commented:

> There was no LTTE women's group like the 'Suthanthira Paravaikal' functioning in the Vanni districts. All the five major groups were directly recruiting women in Vanni. I along with two of my friends were recruited by the TELO and we were taken to Tamil Nadu. We really thought we were joining the LTTE. I was in that TELO base in Tamil

> Nadu for about six weeks. The base was a vast piece of land and there were almost one thousand young people. We were about sixty women and the rest were men. Most of the women were from Jaffna and they were all well-educated. Many had government jobs that they had left to join the TELO movement. At this TELO base we were given political classes by a writer. I cannot remember his name now. There was no arms training at that stage and it was just political lessons. Some of us wanted to go and see the LTTE leader. But we were barred from doing so. Guards stopped us from leaving. We managed to leave. We were attracted to the LTTE by the strict discipline compared to the more relaxed TELO culture. Most of the women at the TELO preferred the TELO because they saw the LTTE as too strict in even letting visitors to see the young women. Most of these other women eventually left the TELO and returned to their families.

One of the six women who left the TELO camp together with Mahes is Vasanthi. The event was described by Vasanthi in one of her writings in 1987.

> In the classes we were taught that our enemy is the LTTE. We were shocked. Eventually we sought a meeting with the LTTE leader and explained our situation. He warned us of the hardships we must face and he gave us a day to think it over and make up our minds on proceeding with the training.

The background to the drama of the six women moving out of the TELO camp to join the first female batch to be trained by the LTTE is likely to be broad. There was protest fasting by these six women at the Chennai Marina beach, after leaving the TELO camp. It is said that the demand from the TELO for the release of two male comrades helped the women to leave the TELO base. The fast was called off quickly and the outcome of their demand remains unclear.

Another woman from Jaffna, Kamala, who arrived in India with her family, was among the nucleus group of nine from Jaffna. Kamala's story about how she was recruited shows the eagerness of Jaffna women to be part of the military training.

Most of Kamala's family had already moved to Tamil Nadu, fearing that their sons and daughters would join the armed movement if they remained in Jaffna. Kamala had refused to move to Tamil Nadu, because she wanted to join the LTTE. Thus Kamala's mother was forced to stay behind with her. Kamala, watching women arriving from Vanni districts to the harbour city of VVT and then shipped off in boats to Tamil Nadu for training, requested the local LTTE leader to send her also for training. He had refused saying that they were not recruiting women from Jaffna. Once she realized staying in Jaffna would not achieve her cherished desire, she told her mother that she was now ready to go to Tamil Nadu. Her mother did not waste a day in moving to Tamil Nadu without realizing Kamala's secret plan to meet Pirapaharan in Tamil Nadu and asked to be recruited. In this Kamala succeeded.

The remaining women in the first batch of ninety to be trained by the LTTE came from the Vanni districts. Vanni consisted of many small agricultural settlements of 20-30 houses. Each settlement was geographically separated from other settlements. Thus the settlement pattern of people in Vanni and its demography is very different from Jaffna. Being an agriculture-based people, with less connection to the Sinhala south, they supported the armed struggle more readily. The presence and the activities of the Sri Lankan military was also much less in the Vanni region. Thus the armed groups moved more freely and the young women in Vanni had greater exposure to the armed groups and they experienced the acceptance of the armed groups by their community. Women in Vanni were not held inside the houses like in Jaffna. These young women are more accustomed to be out in the public working in the fields. All this contributed to the community's greater acceptance of young women enlisting in the armed movements.

The group began training in the hilly area of Sirumalai near Thindukkal in Tamil Nadu. This was a vast area with many huts for the trainees and the trainers. Male pooraalis provided the training for this first batch of female LTTE recruits. Pirapaharan was also at this camp for most of the time. At this training camp, there were about fifteen male pooraalis, in addition to those giving the training, some of these male pooraalis also kept the camp going with supplies and cooking. The women said that Pirapaharan would also join the cooking team that cooked for the women. Food, especially the daily vegetables and the like, was brought up the hill by the locals mostly by horses. The trainees also carried some of the food stuff on their heads. The walk took about one hour and one got a turn once a week.

One incident at the camp site described by the women demonstrates that this was a pioneering phase when established social norms were being broken and the role Pirapaharan played in it. Once a bra belonging to one of the women, which was hanging on a line for drying, had caught the hair of a male pooraali, who tried to walk under the clothes line. The bra was dragged along on his head. There was an uproar among the women. They felt that their clothes should be hung in a private location away from public traffic. Again, Pirapaharan had intervened and said, "If a male is disturbed by the sight of female underwear, he is not fit to be at the camp site". This incident demonstrates two things. It shows the women's subordinated mind-set, where they feel their biological processes and clothing need to be hidden away from the males. It also reveals Pirapaharan's approach to women's matters when he dismisses the women's concerns and demands a relaxed approach from his male comrades.

The toilets were open to the sky with fences on all four sides. Some of the women cried because they did not like the toilets. Stainless steel dinner plates were distributed for the trainees. If one accidentally dropped a plate, the sounds thus made travelled all over the training camp. The person, who dropped the plate, was punished by making him exercise hard. Wasting food also invited punishment. Once, a girl had thrown away a little food. The young women were asked to own up and when no one came forward, all ninety young women were asked to duck walk around the grounds as punishment. During such punishment some women cried because they were not guilty.

The training ran like clockwork according to a schedule. The physical training was very hard and the women cried due to the physical hardship of the training. There were many aspects to the physical training such as, running, climbing and crawling. Beating was also used to urge the young women to continue. One aspect of the training was to test their alertness even during sleep. When an alert signal was sounded the women woke up from sleep put on their shoes and ran to the bunker. Those who ran without shoes were punished. Once inside the bunker stones were thrown at the women to test their reaction. Those who did not take the correct action such as turning and looking in the direction of the stone were punished. Most of the women who had the mental stamina to go through with the training had difficulty building up the physical strength to cope with the training. Sometimes the entire team were made to wait for their meal till all the women had completed the set physical task.

Towards the end of training the physical stamina of most of the women had improved a great deal. Training in Karate and Silambam (a form of Tamil martial art) were also given and these also helped the women to build up their physical stamina. There were fake battles with fake army and those captured by the army were beaten. They were tortured to show what the army would do if it captured them. It also tested their resolve to not divulge information. During such exercises also, some women cried and wanted to go home.

The first batch training was aimed to last for one year. The training for the subsequent batches were only for three months but most often it would last for only one month before they were called out to a battle. The first batch training was intended by Pirapaharan as the testing ground for women. Thus they were given all the training that used to be given to the males. Nothing was missed or spared. The person in charge of the training was a second batch male pooraali Barathy[22] aged around 25. He was a second year undergraduate engineering student, described by the women as extremely strict on the training ground and extremely friendly off the training ground.

Given that it was the testing ground, at the start of the training the women were allowed three days off from training when they got their monthly 'periods'. The women looked forward to these monthly three days break from the gruelling training. It is probably one of those rare instances when women looked forward to having their otherwise unwanted event. However, the trainer, Barathy, consulted a female doctor in Tamil Nadu who advised him that women need not take such breaks and that they were capable of doing everything during that time which they did at other times. Thus Barathy withdrew the three days off option. It was disappointing for the women mainly because they no longer had the excuse to miss the gruelling training from 5.30 am till bed time six days a week.

One woman observed that although theirs was a one-year long training while all the other batches trained for much shorter periods, there was no difference in the performance of the women from the other batches that had a shorter training time. The longer training mainly helped to build up their physical strength, but intelligence, dedication and courage influenced the performance on the battleground. One woman also observed that in the training ground, the twelve Jaffna women in the first batch performed as well as the women from the other districts.

The women had plenty of good clean water because there were waterfalls. Bathing was at the waterfalls around the area. However, they were allowed time for bathing only on Sundays when they also washed their hair. One trainee commented:

> Taking a shower with the noise of the running water and the surrounding scenery is a wonderful experience. Sometimes while showering at the higher platform, we would slip and

> fall down, sometimes even on the heads of those who were showering down below.

Yet, the women also had to cart the water from the water fall, for 500 metres uphill to their camp site for their washing needs. It was a difficult task.

Some of the women in the group set up a Pillaiyaar (god Ganesha) statue under the tree used also as the communication tower. On Sundays after their shower at the waterfall, these women applied holy ash and bindi and put flowers in their hair and prayed at the Pillaiyaar statue. They were nicknamed the Pillaiyaar group by the other women. Some of the other women objected to this practice because such traditional conduct was unbecoming of those engaged in an armed struggle. However, Pirapaharan dismissed their objections saying such things should not be forced on the women but they should come to such decisions on their own. Indeed all the women in the first batch continued to wear their earrings, which is a universal adornment for Tamil women. Later, it was the women themselves, who took the unanimous decision not to wear jewellery including the earrings.

Each Sunday the camp inmates staged performances that they had to prepare during the week. These performances were sometimes staged separately but sometimes the fifteen or so male pooraalis, who were there, would also join in. Mischief and cheating the trainers gave the women a sense of fun. One such incident was recalled by one:

> We had to walk to another place for the shooting training. For this we were each given a dummy grenade which we had to keep with us and take for the shooting training and bring it back with us. Once, my friend and I forgetfully left our dummy grenade at the training grounds. When we realized it, we ran back to collect it. The leader was there and he pulled us up. As punishment he decided to make us carry heavy stones with us all the time. Ponnamaan chose the stones weighing about 20 kilograms each that we were to carry. One aspect of this type of punishment was the explanation that had to be

given to each and every person about why they were given this punishment. To avoid carrying the rocks to and from the walk to the shooting training site, we put in place a scheme. We chose two more rocks that looked similar to the ones given to us. We would always walk the distance as the last two people in the group and leave our rocks at one end and walk free to the other end. There we will pick up the other two rocks that we kept hidden and carry it to the training site. A similar swap will be made on the return trek. However, we still had to carry the rocks at the shooting training site and around our living area for one week. We were not discovered till the end.

Sometimes a wild buffalo would be shot. The young women were called upon to help with the cleaning and preparation of the meat. The meat was dry cooked. The women would sometimes hide some pieces of the dry meat in their pockets. They shared this with the other women at night. The leftover meat in their pockets was attacked by the mice ruining their pockets in the process. Pirapaharan nick-named these women 'karuvaaddu kalli' (dry-meat-thieves).

Also around the area, there were horticulture farms for pineapple and jack fruit. The local people around the area were poor people and they were very friendly with the young women. The young women would go there to collect firewood. The locals gave them fruits to eat. After an incident where two locals had committed suicide and were found hanging, the young women were frightened and reduced their jaunts into these areas.

Pirapaharan always believed the women when their stories differed from the version given by the men. Once, three of the women wanted to go to Thindukkal. So they claimed they had toothache and needed to see the dentist. Pirapaharan agreed and a day was fixed for them to go. Not that the women had money in hand. In Thindukkal there were two or three houses ready to receive the pooraalis who came down for treatment. One of these houses was just for the young women. The people in this house would get ice-cream for the women who had come down. One of the male pooraali, at the training camp, told Pirapaharan that the women only wanted to go to have ice-cream and that they had no toothache. Pirapaharan, who always trusted the women, sent them anyway. The young women did see the dentist to pull teeth and also ate ice-cream.

This first batch training lasted for one year and the group graduated in 1985. They were forced to stay on at Sirumalai for another six months owing to delays in returning back home. The ninety trainees were divided into six teams of fifteen. Four teams remained in the military division. Two of the teams were allocated to the financial section. From the financial section some later went to the political division.

Initially the male commanders of Jaffna and Vanni districts, Kittu and Mathaya refused to take the young women under their command. Many of the women said that Kittu, the Jaffna commander, resisted enlisting women. They tell stories on how hard Pirapaharan tried to convince him otherwise and succeeded in this.

It was, Victor, the commander of the Mannar district who eventually agreed to take the first batch women under his command. The entire team landed in small numbers in Mannar. The very first military engagement, of the first batch women, took place in Adampan in Mannar in October 1986 under Victor's command. Sadly, in this Adampan, battle Victor was killed. Anoja, one of the women under his command, was quoted in Adele's book:

> Lt. Col. Victor fell wounded. The women lifted him and carried him to a safe place. He was bleeding heavily from a bullet wound in the chest. As we were carrying him the army started firing at us from all directions. Another bullet hit Lt.Col.Victor in the leg and side. Amazingly none of us were injured. We put him down and his head was on my lap. We tried to stop the bleeding. Lt. Col. Victor tried to talk. Suddenly, he grabbed my wrist firmly and quietly fell back. He was dead.

Following the Mannar battles, half of the team were sent to Kilinochchi to function under Mathaya. When Kilinochchi was taken by the Lankan military, most of the team moved to Jaffna. At this point the women were still under the command of male leaders. When the women arrived in Jaffna, Pirapaharan was not in Tamil Eelam. The other male leaders in Jaffna instructed the women not to move in public in their shirts and pants, though they were allowed to wear shirts and pants inside their camps. They were also given skirts to be worn whenever they left the camp for outside work. When Pirapaharan arrived and wanted to meet the first batch women they thus went to see him in their skirts. Pirapaharan inquired about this new outfit and the women told him of the rule to be followed while in Jaffna. He had dismissed it saying the women need not follow any rules enforced by the men. Thus the women started moving around in shirts and pants after this.

By 2009, seventeen of these ninety women had been killed in battles and seven of them remained in Vanni, while the rest of them were spread around the world. Vasanthi was one of those who remained in Vanni. She was then being cared for in a home because she was disabled. She was among the thousands killed in the final genocidal assault by Lanka. It is apt to cite a piece Vasanthi wrote in January 1989 in the LTTE publication, *Tamil Eelam*, about her comrade Imelda who was killed by the Indian forces. About Imelda she commented:

> You would lament about our society that does not regard us, who have completed training, as respectable women. You would say that this must be changed and all the women of Tamil Eelam must participate in the struggle in some way. That change will come only gradually. I reflect on what you said and see that you had departed us when your dream is materializing...[23]

5

From Suthanthira Paravaikal to LTTE Pooraali

The failure of the parliamentary means of gaining Tamil rights had translated into a powerful urge among the younger Tamils to militarily confront the Sri Lankan military as the means of gaining independence. The role of the SP, on the other hand, was to work among the people by sharing their hardships and helping to alleviate it. This work did not earn prestige among the Tamils as did the act of direct military confrontation with the enemy. The culture that evolved elevated those who took up arms at the expense of those who worked with the people. Among the five main armed groups, this culture gained most currency within the LTTE. It had some negative repercussions later as the armed struggle ground on.

Rani, who was an SP activist remembered her eagerness:

> Initially, women were not recruited openly in Jaffna. In fact, we at the SP must have received the training in the first batch that trained in Tamil Nadu. We had been working actively from 1984. People in Jaffna were not prepared at that time to accept women getting involved in public activities. We cannot achieve 'political freedom' without 'social freedom' or rather 'women's freedom'. To bring about that change women must also carry arms. There was nothing available to understand women's freedom. No television or reading material. We had to inform the people about the women's rights through dramas, speeches and publications. It was only through these activities that people became aware and were ready to accept women's participation.

Even before the SP women were given training, some of the women from Vadamaradchi were stationed with guns and grenades to guard security posts surrounding military camps. Each such post would have about five trained male pooraalis and two trained female pooraalis from the first batch and one SP woman. Rani observed:

> We met the LTTE leader once and we argued with him regarding why we were not given training. We argued that we could also do what the boys did. That is why we from Vadamaradchi area were put with the first batch women to guard security posts. We had courage, we did not have fear. That is because we have seen a lot, especially what was happening to the women by the Lanka military. We had also seen the activities of the male pooraalis, how they were functioning. They visited our homes regularly. All of it produced a strong emotional attraction for battles. All of us in the SP from the Vadamaradchi area were keen and active like this.

By 1987, the Vadamaradchi region, which includes Pirapaharan's birthplace, had become the main operation centre for the LTTE. In fact the LTTE had such control of this region that it was out of bounds for the Sri Lankan military. The Sri Lankan military launched a major operation, 'Operation Liberation', in May 1987 to seize control of this region from the LTTE. The effect of this first ever major conventional military operation against the LTTE was felt throughout the Jaffna peninsula. The threat to the young men and women who had worked actively for the LTTE as non-members became too high. Most of the leading SP women who were well known in the community had to leave home for their own safety. More than one hundred of them had gathered in three houses in Kalviyankaadu near Jaffna city. These houses had become de facto LTTE bases for the SP women who were to be sent for military training, although at this time no decision was made to train the SP women. The SP women from the Vadamaradchi region, although some of them were well known SP leaders, were trapped by the military operation and were unable to leave the region and join the other SP women at Kalviyankaadu.

Rani described how she and her friends managed to escape from her home area to join the group of SP women who were preparing for training that was about to start in the Kilali-Chavakachcheri region,

> SL Army had encircled Vadamaradchi. I went from house to house to ask all the SP women to get ready to go for the training. One night we walked with one of my uncles. To camouflage the group, my uncles carried a basket of vegetables and we all wore the traditional outfit, the skirt and blouse. We cut through the military encirclement with a male pooraali team in front and arrived in Chavakachcheri. We arrived at night and met Thileepan. We walked more through the same night with Thileepan to arrive at the training camp in Kilali. There were others from the SP there, all awaiting the training. We knew most of them because we used to meet them during SP meetings. The next morning we put up the sheds for us to live. The posts and thatched coconut leaves were already there. That took one day and the next day the training started. One of the women had to leave for home because she was asthmatic and 99 of us took the training.

The most noted SP women, close to one hundred of them, who were in Kalviyankaadu houses were selected for training. The remaining women as well as those who could not make it to Kalviyankaadu were asked to continue with the SP work. One woman, who had arrived in this house keen to take the training but was not selected for the training was Kalai. Like others in her shoes, she was told to work for the SP for some time before taking the training. She along with a few others were accommodated in a house in Mallakam and were asked to work among the uprooted people in the camps in Mallakam. Thileepan gave them the instructions and advice on how they had to proceed with this work. They would meet Thileepan every week at the Kalviyankaadu base to discuss progress and problems. The women took care of the various needs of the uprooted people which included their medical needs and hygiene; ensuring that the children attended school; and also ensuring that they received the rations due to them as uprooted people. Kalai commented that they received great praise from Thileepan for their work.

Some of the other women who were also not chosen to take the second batch training recalled with bitterness about the choice to include two friends, Shenuka and Ajanthi, in the second batch training. They felt bitter because unlike them these two women had not worked in the SP movement. While the culture of SP women had evolved by sharing hardships with the people, these two women, who came from the wealthier section of the Jaffna society, were unaware of the SP movement. Because they appeared ill prepared for the hardships of armed struggle, a source house was specifically selected to expose them to the reality of the hardships they would have to face as a pooraali[24].

As the 'Operation Liberation' continued in Vadamaradchi, the training of the second batch of women began in Kilali. About 10-15 of the women who were trained in the first batch imparted the training. According to many of the trainees the facilities at the training base were reasonable. The food was nutritious and given only in measured amounts suitable for training. Milk and mung beans, or rice kanchi were given for breakfast. For lunch it would be one of eggs, or fish and at times meat would also be served. According to the women, Pirapaharan usually took direct interest in the quality of food given during the training period. Many of the women suffered due to lack of food choice. Vegetarians also suffered because at times there was only a non-vegetarian food. The vegetarians found it hard to get used to the non-vegetarian food and some would vomit when they forced themselves to eat it. Water was a problem but water was delivered by tanks and it was rationed. There were people appointed to organize this. The training was supposed to be for three months. As in the case of the first batch who were trained in Tamil Nadu, the women cried due to the hardship of training. Some hid behind trees to avoid doing the full 20 laps that was required. One month into the training, the Indian military landed in the island and the training prematurely came to an end.

Most of the 10-15 first batch women, who gave training to the second batch of women, had already been gradually taken away for battles with the Sri Lankan military. The second batch women were now taken to the village of Suthumalai where Pirapaharan gave a speech about the Indo-Lanka accord. At the end of this, the women were told to go back to their homes and continue the SP work. The SP women felt lost and orphaned. They could not consider the possibility of going back home after all the work they had put into the liberation struggle. Santha described how she and a few others stood on the road considering their plight:

> Mathaya had told us to go home if we wished. A few of us stood on the road feeling like orphans unwilling to go home after working for a goal for so many years. Some did go home because they were disillusioned. The SP women were affected psychologically. In the end Soosai took charge of us.

Eventually the women who refused to go home were accommodated in bases that were set up for them. Around forty of the women were accommodated in a base in Chavakachcheri. Some women were accommodated in a house called Kalviyankaadu. Some of the Vadamaradchi women set up a base for themselves in Vadamaradchi. All the women from the second batch, those who went home as well as those who stayed in these bases discarded their uniforms and went back to wearing skirts and tops.

Nila commented thus about the base in Chavakachcheri:

> Thinesh (later Tamilselvan) was given the responsibility of ensuring we were supplied with our requirements. Otherwise he had very little to do with us. Since we were all unarmed and were new to the area, he was also given the responsibility of protecting us in the event of an attack.

A few weeks after the second batch training was prematurely stopped, Thileepan, the driving force behind the SP, decided to protest fast putting five demands to the Indian forces. The SP women now came out in saris to campaign support for Thileepan's fasting. Nila comments:

> Just before he started the fast, he asked me and a few others from SP to come and see him. But we did not go, feeling discomfort at the idea of Thileepan going on fasting till death. When Thileepan was well into the fasting, we went to see him. When we went later Thileepan's condition had deteriorated. We did not expect that level of deterioration. We thought he was only doing a protest fast. We did not think he would die. He talked to us about how we should continue to function. He said that he was entrusting the job to us and that we should continue the work as we had planned.

Thileepan died on 26th September after fasting for twelve days without food or water. Following Thileepan's fasting to death, another incident also deeply touched the women at the Chavakachcheri base. Kumarappa-Pulendran group of twelve visited the women at the Chavakachcheri base. The group of twelve were to embark on a trip to Trincomalee by sea. During that trip they were arrested by the Sri Lankan Navy. Protesting their arrest and their proposed transfer to Colombo, under the Sri Lankan military, while the Indian forces were supposedly on a peace keeping mission, the group of twelve took their lives by biting the cyanide capsule. When the group of twelve visited the women at the Chavakachcheri base they had a meal with the women. They discussed with the women the evolving situation with the Indian forces and warned the women that the situation could become worse. Once they left, Pirapaharan also discussed the changing situation with the women.

The war between the LTTE and the Indian forces broke out in October 1987. Rani recalled how she took herself to the war with the Indian forces.

> One day my friend and I watched the very first battle between the LTTE and the Indian forces. We were going on our bicycles. We rode past my father who warned us to be careful because the Indian forces were out. As we went, a vehicle came at high speed from a lane in front of us and another vehicle drove past us. Immediately there was shooting. That was the very first battle with the Indians. We went back to our base, wore jeans and took the rifle, because we knew the battle had started. We then received the command from Soosai anna to come to his base. There he told us that we could join the Jaffna battle if we wished. He dug out the weapons and distributed them. We then went to the Jaffna battle. I was in the Kokkuvil-Kondavil area.

All the women from the second batch were now called upon for the battle near the Jaffna University. Both sides faced heavy losses in the initial battles. Among the LTTE casualties were many—around 20—of the first and second batch female pooraalis. Santha commented that the battle with the Indian forces was mostly about shooting and running away.

The first female Maaveerar in the LTTE, Malathi, killed in Kopay, was also among those killed in the battle with the Indian forces. Malathi was from the first batch of female trainees who trained in Tamil Nadu in 1984. Janani of Senchchoolai fame, who was also from the first batch of female pooraalis, was quoted in Adele's book as follows:

> We were in our bunkers firing at the army. Hundreds of Indian troops had jumped out of their vehicles and were firing as they moved towards us. Mortar shells were exploding everywhere. We knew the army was advancing quickly. Malathi was shot in both legs. She could not move and was bleeding profusely. Realizing that she was mortally wounded, she swallowed cyanide. A decision had been made to withdraw because we were heavily outnumbered. Another woman Vijee and I went over to carry Malathi. Malathi refused to come with us. She begged us to leave her and asked us to withdraw. Nevertheless, we lifted Malathi and carried her and when we arrived at a safe place she was dead.

Kamala, from the first batch was also injured in her chest in the battle with the Indian forces. Her injury was serious enough to plan to send her to Tamil Nadu for treatment. However, Kamala refused to go to India. She was taken to Moolai hospital where the doctors said she was too seriously injured to survive any surgery. The male pooraali who took her to the hospital told the doctors to go ahead and she was thus treated there. She had to vacate the hospital the following day because the Indian forces were nearing the hospital. She was then looked after in a private home belonging to a supporter. This was the manner in which injured pooraalis were cared for those days.

Eventually the LTTE decided to withdraw into the Vanni jungles. The withdrawal took place in small groups. Rani described her arrival in the Vanni jungles.

> Then our leader told us to withdraw. We went to Puthukkudiyiruppu and from there walked to Manalaaru. We arrived in batches. We received orders about who was to go where. My team that was with Gracy Anna was told to go to Manalaaru. We arrived in Visuvamadu where Mathaya anna talked to us and then they took us into the jungle.

The LTTE group that withdrew into the Vanni jungle split into two main sections. One group arrived in Manalaaru where Pirapaharan was located and the other in Palamoddai where Mathaya was located. Around ten women from the first and second batch training were among the LTTE members left behind in Jaffna charged with the task of continuing the work there. For over two years from 1988-89 the LTTE was restricted to the Vanni jungles.

The few women who were left behind in Jaffna carried out work that could not be done by male comrades such as collecting intelligence and putting up posters. After the LTTE withdrew, the SOLT group did not have LTTE coordinators. The senior students in the SOLT re-organized themselves and continued with some of their activities. They too put up notices and helped in the movement of the armed members, and helped to shift weapons. Many SOLT members were killed by the Indian forces for their activities. One SOLT member recalled how they went door knocking at midnight asking people to gather at a junction for a protest. The LTTE did not recruit from SOLT but always encouraged them to continue with their studies. However, once the harassment of the Indian forces intensified and some SOLT members were killed, others sneaked out to the Vanni jungle and enlisted with the LTTE. Thurga, the Commander of the Sothiya regiment, one of the two major women's regiments of the LTTE, and Barathy who was an SP activist during this time were among those who went thus to the Vanni jungle.

6

Making of the Military Women: 1988-1990

Earlier sections have already noted the necessity of military training for the women for their own safety, the prestige afforded to this training and the nature of the training given to the first two batches of women. The two years spent in the Vanni jungle during the presence of the Indian forces in the homeland provided a unique opportunity to focus only on this military aspect. The group that went to the Manalaaru jungle with Pirapaharan focused on the military aspect. The other group in Palamoddai under Mathaya was meant to focus on the socio-political aspects but still removed from the people. This second group was occupied with publishing. It continued to publish SP issues as well as another general publication called *Unarvu*.

These two years in the Manalaaru jungle with accompanying shortages of vital necessities like water and the constant threat from the Indian forces and resulting frequent battles did create a special character in the women. One woman noted:

> This created greater tolerance of differences and greater sense of togetherness among us. We worked together better, ignoring minor problems and differences.

Initially around 30-40 women arrived in the Manalaaru jungles. More new recruits joined the group over the following two years and the numbers swelled and reached nearly 200. They were trained in four more batches referred to in the LTTE history as 3rd (8 women), 4th (59 women), 5th (approximately

100 women) and 6th (approximately 100 women) batches. One of the women to arrive at the start Rani commented:

> In Manalaaru, at the start there was difficulty in obtaining everything. Mathy (Pirapaharan's wife) collected old sarongs for us to use as sanitary pads. But the leader would always work hard to fulfil our needs. This problem lasted for about three weeks."

Another woman Kavitha who trained in the 5th batch said:

> Items like tea, sugar, milk or oil were unthinkable. Even starchy food was in short supply. One time kerosene was accidentally poured into a sack of rice. We still ate it. Meat of animals hunted in the jungle provided some food but it was difficult to get sufficient quantities of meat to satisfy our hunger. This kind of jungle life and training was only till the 6th batch.

Adele in her book also noted the hardships:

> They worked and struggled to create a habitable environment out of wild virgin jungle and to transform the hostile wilderness into an enduring ally. ... Both the male and female cadres worked day and night digging out trenches, constructing bunkers, putting up huts and tents and clearing pathways.... Water - that vital resource for human survival - was very scarce in the jungle but it was available deep underground... could only be acquired by digging deep wells.

The constant threat of attacks by the Indian forces was another aspect of life during this time. Adele described what they faced:

> ...From June 1988 the Indian army launched a series of operations codenamed 'Operation Checkmate'. In these operations the Indian army singled out the LTTE bases in the Alampil jungles. Massive aerial and artillery bombardment was launched. Hundreds of tons of powerful bombs and artillery shells were rained down, day and night, on LTTE positions...

Many of the women credited Pirapaharan with a technique that built confidence in them. He organized tasks or training either in parallel or together with men to experiment/ demonstrate that women can do what men can, even when the need is physical strength. He organized these so that the women could see for themselves that they could do as well as the men. Without this immediate comparison being available, even if women try as hard as they can, it is not readily visible to them what they can also achieve compared to the men.

One woman remembered how they were assigned the task of digging a well in parallel to the men. Pirapaharan would observe the two teams in operation and tell the women that they must work harder and lying to them that the men were doing better. Only when the task was finished the women realized that they had done much better than the men. This appears to be a technique that Pirapaharan used in these early days. Except for paucity in menstruation the women noticed no negative effects on their health as a result of these extreme physical exertions.

In 1989 an extremely hard training was organized for a group of selected men and women. There were 10-15 women and 60 men. They were all chosen for their physical abilities. The trainers were instructed not to make the training regimen less severe for the women. Thus the training was on an equal footing. All those who were undergoing training came together for meetings, shooting training and for practice attacks. But the training was held separately though the men and women were at a visible distance from each other. The training became a healthy competition between the men and women. The important point that must be noted is that these 10-15 women were sent for this training with men who were also selected for their physical strength. Pirapaharan may have used this as a test to see how much women can be pushed to be equal to men.

During this special training the women cried due to the extremely hard training. They had to continue the training even while they were menstruating. The women in the end did perform equal to men. Later it was observed that these women were different and had more self-confidence. Other women who worked with them later in various tasks found them to be inspirational. They handled the most difficult physical work, like clearing the jungle or digging a well, with playfulness, encouraging others too to be playful while doing the task. This made others also view the task as a site for play and humour. The result was that the task was carried out with fun and confidence. Be it digging wells, putting up huts for habitation or other purposes, these ten women were leaders for the other women. They knew the techniques needed for building more complex huts which earlier was considered to be the knowledge that belonged only to the men. Eventually junior men had to come and learn some of these techniques from women. These ten women then may well have been the spring of confidence from which the women who followed drew on.

One of the women who received this special training said:

> Our leader said women are wiser than men though men might be faster. When men were ready to withdraw women persisted in pushing forward. When both are together there is more cooperation and the strengths of the two genders complement each other. When we were training, even women's matters like monthly periods did not seem an issue at that time. But today we make a fuss over it and say I cannot cook because of the period and the like. When we were training we ignored these as minor issues. Today we have become family women.

Only after this training had proved that women could stand alone, women were allowed to go it alone and set up their own bases and be responsible for their own security. They dug their own wells, built their own huts, ensured their own security, organized their own supplies for which sometimes they had to trek through jungles, and planned their own work. The ten women played a major role in this paradigm shift in women's role. Till then the LTTE leader kept the women in his camp under his supervision. All the facilities needed for the women mentioned were set up by the men. Pirapaharan could not let the women go it alone until he had confidence in their abilities to protect themselves. Otherwise he would have taken flak from the wider society for not protecting the women. There were many incidents after this where women in great danger took strategic decisions to ensure their safety from enemy soldiers.

The lessons women were taught is that if persevered they could do anything that the men could do. One view point is that the confidence in their physical strength also contributed to the women's confidence in their mental and intellectual strength. Though the latter have already been proven at many levels at the global level, at an individual level and in that cultural context proving their physical strength appeared to have enhanced the confidence of the women and may well be a technique to be taken note of.

Women in the Manalaaru jungles thus progressed to setting up their own military structure completely independent of men. In the LTTE history, the women's military units turned out to be the only women's units that did not have to report to any other male leaders except Pirapaharan. These women only structures facilitated younger women to develop their own skills in administration, decision-making and leadership.

During this phase in the Manalaaru jungle, young men and women lived and worked in close proximity. One couple developed a sexual relationship unknown to their comrades. The girl concerned became pregnant. The conditions under which the group was living, the secrecy of the location, and the potential damage to their profile as a disciplined group, meant the couple could not be sent back to the community. The group was called upon to decide on what had to be done. The decision to execute the couple was taken unanimously with one dissension. Adele alluded to this:

> Crucial to the successful outcome of the training programme and the functioning of the LTTE is the maintenance of

> discipline in the cadres. From the outset of the basic training programme, classes are given setting out clearly the codes of conduct of the LTTE and the nature of punishment. This discipline is vigorously maintained by all those in charge of the LTTE cadres.

This action and another similar action a few years later is remembered by the members and probably contributed to the LTTE's development as a highly disciplined movement. In this second incident three women from the Sea Tigers unit were given similar punishment for inappropriate behaviour with civilian males who were admitted to their base to carry out some work. In this case the males were also executed publicly. Besides these two incidents the LTTE women said there were no other similar incidents where members were given such punishment.

The military training of women continued for the rest of the LTTE history in new batches. The Manalaaru training camp was complemented by re-establishing the Kilali training camp where the second batch initially began its training. Women continued to join through many avenues and their training continued in parallel in both camps.

The drive of the women to excel in the military sector is exemplified by one woman. Rani was injured and unable to walk for two years. She spent those two years studying politics. She went back to battles with her disability with an assistant to do what she could not do due to the disability. Rani explained why the military aspect was attractive to her:

> Battle is attractive because of the close relationships with fellow female cadres, away from society with all the associated pressures, away from males and we are on our own about to take a challenge, the knowledge that we are doing something unusual, the excitement and pride in collecting the weapons left by the enemy.

She was injured again and left battle lines for good. In due course the women's military sector expanded to form two main regiments, the Malathi regiment and the Sothiya regiment in 1996. The Malathi regiment was the mother regiment and it took its history from the beginning. Its military history is recorded in a book[25] in Tamil. The history of the Sothiya regiment started from 1996 when the mother regiment was split into two because it had grown too large.

Military Leaders Sothiya, Vithusha and Thurga

Other military sections evolved. One legendary women's military section was the Siruthai regiment. Its battle successes also made impressive history. Yet for reasons of secrecy, it has not been much talked about. There were also a women's Sea Tiger unit, a female Military Intelligence unit, a female Land Mine unit, a female Black Tiger unit and so on.

The benefits of military training was encapsulated in the comment made by Meena:

> When we have weapons in hand and the confidence in handling it we felt we could do anything. I understood what unarmed means when I was standing in Vadduvahal in May 2009.

Geopolitics-4

In 1987, the Indian forces in the island tried to re-arm TELO without much success. TELO was the preferred group for the Indian establishment which also explains but not justifies the earlier killing of TELO fighters by the LTTE. The TELO maintained an ambivalent position in relation to the LTTE for some years after. But starting from the mid-1990s, it began to take an increasingly pro-LTTE stand. In 2001, it joined the coalition of Tamil political parties, the TNA.

In 1989, while the Indian forces were still stationed in Tamil Eelam, Rajini Thiranagama, a vociferous critic of both the Indian forces and the LTTE, was shot and killed.

Indian forces withdrew from the island in 1990 when the Sri Lankan government and the LTTE together asked them to leave.

Soon after UTHR, a self-proclaimed human rights body, published the book *Broken Palmyra*. One of its authors claimed to be Rajini Thiranagama, who was killed in 1989. UTHR continued to publish reports portraying the LTTE very negatively. For this, it was much admired and appreciated in the mainstream discourse until 2009. In 2007, two of the UTHR architects received the Martin Ennals Award for Human Rights Defenders in which Amnesty International is a key player.

7

SP Tries Revival: 1990-1995

The last two chapters noted how the arrival of the Indian troops propelled militarism and its success among the women. The time is 1990 and it is the moment when LTTE re-enters Jaffna following the departure of the Indian military. It is a turning point in the struggle waged by the LTTE. Till then, the LTTE had not controlled a large enough region where they could function without the harassment of an outside military. For the first time in its history, the LTTE had more or less the entire responsibility to administer Jaffna. The LTTE women too saw this as a milestone from their perspective of working towards progressive societal changes. They had the political space to act out their plans which they had absorbed during their time as SP members, with the confidence they had gained in the Vanni jungles encouraged by Pirapaharan. This chapter will trace the development of activism among the women after the death of Thileepan and the departure of the Indian military. This was the period of impressive growth of Tamil female militarism and the struggle to revive the SP activism.

When the Indian military left, in the brief period of peace that followed, the LTTE began to perform the functions of a government in Tamil areas. LTTE managed all administration processes through the political wing, which it had formed around this time. The planning for agriculture, environment and pollution, housing and the banking system was described by a Diaspora Tamil visitor, Ethiveerasingam[26]. It gives the flavour of the process at that time. Excerpts from that description:

> The LTTE administration has prepared blueprints ready to build airports, seaports, town centres and a comprehensive road and railway network, schools and other buildings in the north-east before the current hostilities started in April 1995.
>
> The LTTE administration in 1990 formed a committee of specialists from the University, government departments, private sector and citizens to plan and rebuild the Jaffna city. The committee completed its work under the chairmanship of the then Vice-Chancellor, Prof. A. Thurairajah, a civil engineer. The plan and architect drawing were presented by the LTTE infrastructure team at a meeting of the DAC in Kilinochchi in 1994 where I was present. It is a modern plan for a destroyed ancient city. During my stay, a committee was elected to plan the Kilinochchi and Mankulam towns, which completed the draft in April 1995. The committee had full freedom and all assistance to hold meetings for people to present their views and recommendations.
>
> This was the standard approach of the LTTE in all matters concerning the development of the north. I have had the privilege of examining the final draft of the document. The final draft was similar to the first draft in cost (Rs. 39.9 billion) but had more details and contained a section giving the summary of the proposal presented by the LTTE for approximately Rs. 100 billion. I have not seen this level of mass participation of citizens in planning processes of governmental function anywhere else. In the south such a process is highly centralized.

During the presence of the Indian troops, while a large number of females received military training in the Manalaaru jungle, another group of women who were part of the SP under Thileepan had moved into the Palamoddai jungle, headed by Mathaya, on the other side of the A9 road. The work of these women during the presence of the Indian forces was mainly publishing. The magazines were handwritten and printed using manual operated printing press. There was a magazine called *Unarvu* produced by the men and women in this group and the women also continued the publication of the SP magazine.

A political party, which later became known as the political division, was formed after the departure of the Indian military, to be headed by Mathaya. Around the same time, a team of 150 women were selected, from the Manalaaru camp and the Palamoddai camp, to be sent to Jaffna as one team. The LTTE leader had talked to the 150 women before they left for Jaffna. According to one woman in this group, he had also talked to a small group from this team and he had suggested Santha should be in charge of the women's political division and Barathy should be the head of SOLT. This team arrived in Point Pedro and was staying in two houses. Santha, who was initially at the Manalaru camp under Pirapaharan and later went to the Palamoddai camp, came to meet this group of 150 women. She selected 30 women to work in the women's section of the political division. All the women at that time thought that Santha was going to be the head of the women's political division.

One woman, who was among the 150 women who arrived from Manalaaru, had just met Santha. Santha had selected her and three or four more women to work in the SP publication. She says she learnt a lot from Santha who was well read, single-minded and sincere. When the 30 women selected by Santha arrived in Jaffna, they learnt that it was Jeya and not Santha who was going to be the head of the women's political division. Also, instead of Barathy, Aravindan, a male was appointed as the head of SOLT by Mathaya. Both these appointments disappointed the SP women nurtured by Thileepan.

Jeya who obtained her training in the first batch in Tamil Nadu was one of the handful women from Jaffna in the first batch. She was educated at Jaffna University and had not been under Thileepan's guidance and thus lacked the experience of working among the downtrodden people and receiving the revolutionary ideals that Thileepan imparted to the SP women. She also stayed behind in Jaffna during the time of the Indian forces and thus lacked experience of sharing hardships in the jungle with fellow comrades. All these may have coloured the way she viewed how to take the women's struggle forward. However, women who joined after Jeya became the head of the women's political wing rated Jeya highly as a leader. The overall leader for the women at this time was also another woman from the first batch.

The SP women who had ideals of women's liberation now had no one leader to fall behind. However, Jeya divided the women's political section into many divisions: CWDR, CWR, SP Publication and District Heads. More women were active in the 'Arts and Culture', Police and Justice Divisions. Many of the earlier SP activists were either in charge of the divisions or otherwise active in it. The activities of these divisions under the earlier SP activists made massive waves in the society on women's issues. Some of these divisions that were created and how they affected the society is described below. What follows is only a very brief description of these endeavours. Each of them could be expanded by those who have had extensive first-hand experience in it. Hopefully, for the benefit of the future generations, such early activists will write them down one day before the memories of it fades.

When asked to talk about the political work they carried out among civilian women, it became clear that the LTTE women had two different views of what they meant by 'political work'. One that these women proudly talked about was to do with taking part in the hardships of the people. According to the women who joined the LTTE before 1990, this was the focus of their political work. Many women said that after 1990 there was a gradual deterioration and later this tended to be 'preaching' to the people. Some of the women thought that it was the lack of focus on people's hardships that may have necessitated forced recruitment from 2006 onwards.

Barathy

Janani of Senchchoolai

Thamilini

Civil Leaders

One woman described how the LTTE leader described political work to a group of women entering Jaffna after the departure of the Indian forces:

> Learn to love the people. Help them in small ways and when in charge in big ways too. This is how our leader talked to those going to do to political work. A political pooraali is one who shares the hardships and tragedies of the people. When you come across prostitution do not think of punishing them. But examine the reasons and find alternate solutions. Create awareness in them about the damage. One needs to spend time with them and their children. We came with these ideas and we were sent to different areas. One of the women Amuthini would come for each monthly meeting with a plan. For example, to set up small-scale cottage industries like a chicken farm, rope making and the like. She would come with details of women in hardships, widows and so on. But Jeya would dismiss them as unpractical.

Another LTTE woman denied that the heightened level of safety that women felt in the LTTE administered regions were due to the arms the LTTE members carried. She asserted:

> All governments have arms and the LTTE which was running a state like administration too had the same arms. Unlike most states, the LTTE administration reached the bottom strata of the society. Representatives of the LTTE administration reached this strata on a regular basis. It was this kind of administration that caused the positive changes like women's safety. Also outside contact was very limited. There were no phones and no television. Even outside imports were limited. People were involved in their own manufacturing of all essential and non-essential stuff. This enriched the inter-dependent production relationships. The activities of the multinational corporations and government policies these days weaken these inter-dependent relationships. With this weakened relationship, unity which strengthens a society, is also weakened. Each person has become a single unit with none or at best very weakened relationships.
>
> When the LTTE was active, a sense of nationhood was infused into people and this also strengthened the relationships

and the unity. This environment also urged a self-reflecting thinking person that enriched the society.

Women police, the presence of women in public space was a positive sign. It also encouraged to women to take their issues to police women. Even morally it gave strength to all women.

CWDR

Santha, who was considered by fellow women, the one with the most profound awareness of the societal ills, mostly acted independently of Jeya. She started a women's development organization, which functioned with a high level of independence. It reached the bottom strata of women and worked to uplift their situation in life, by endeavouring to give them an independent income by developing low key local level industries such as rope, cloth and paper making as well as agricultural endeavours. Santha independently researched and developed some manufacturing techniques suitable for these industries that could give employment to women. Santha started making rope from coconut husk and making recycled paper. Santha's organization also did farming. Under Shantha an NGO, CWDR, was created to give an acceptable face to the outside world regarding the women's work that was being done. Another SP activist Aruna was in charge of this NGO. Eventually the entire organization took on the name CWDR and it continued to function as an NGO in LTTE administered regions. These industries that were started by Santha also continued as part of the CWDR employment giving schemes till 2008.

At the time of the launch of CWDR, it also took in orphaned children into its care. Efforts were made to identify children who needed such care. After about two years the new institution, Senchcholai, was created for the children in need, which was under Janani's management. Much later, Senchcholai was split into two institutions for the boys and the girls. Senchcholai remaining as the girls' home and a different home for the boys.

CWDR continued to branch out to other parts of Tamil Eelam and several such branches were created for each district of Tamil Eelam. It, however, did not rise to the heights hoped for by Santha.

SOLT

SOLT had existed prior to the Indian involvement and its leader was Murali. Thileepan, who was also the Jaffna district head, had an active role in SOLT. It was not exclusively a women's division but included men and women. Murali was killed in battle with the Indian forces. When the LTTE re-entered Jaffna after the departure of the Indian forces, the LTTE leader had appointed a woman, Barathy, to be the leader of SOLT. However, Mathaya is supposed to have demoted her to be the second in charge of SOLT and replaced her with a male. Barathy soon left SOLT unhappy about the students' conduct. After leaving SOLT, Barathy was made second to Jeya for the Women's Political Division. In this role, Barathy was instrumental in setting up corrective farms for female prisoners and their children and did a great job of this. The women prisoners in the corrective farms earned money which was credited to their account and their children were sent to school. Barathy, also distanced herself from Jeya because of the style difference between the SP activists and the first batch women.

CWR (Centre for Women's Research)

When CRW was launched, Barathy was made in charge. Under her, CWR had developed a large library. It also published a regular magazine called *Naattru* which continued publication till 2008. Barathy, who joined the LTTE in 1989, was killed in 1992 when she accidentally entered Lankan military area. Some women members have reservations as to why she entered Lankan military area and even suspect sabotage. Pirapaharan had ambitious plans for Barathy as a promising leader. One woman said that if Santha and Barathy were given positions of power they would have created a great social revolution. The poem by Barathy written in 1993 in Chapter 10 demonstrates her depth of insight.

After Barathy's death, CWR's notable work was a campaign against dowry practice and dealing with women who needed a helping hand on legal matters. The campaign against dowry practice is described in the next section. After the exodus from Jaffna, CWR did not carry out any further research. Other than this campaign, CWR ended up mostly handling counselling for family issues. CWR took up issues where women who got into trouble with law and needed a helping hand. These were cases involving women that were not readily resolved in courts and were thus handed over to CWR to be dealt with through counselling. One of the common issues that CWR handled till the end was the issue of male-female couple relationships. When a woman was abandoned by a man after a romantic relationship, whether it was: just holding hands, taking part in a physical sexual relationship or making her pregnant, it was a serious matter in that social context. Such women faced a bleak future. The entire female LTTE section took it upon on itself to ensure that such women were protected for life. Both the courts that evolved under the LTTE and CWR played an active role in protecting women thus 'abandoned'.

CWR took charge of them when the courts could not resolve their issue. All the court files related to the case were handed to CWR. In effect, it acted like a private agent. Women of CWR held the men concerned at the police cell and provided counselling to make the male accept his paternity of the child, so that the child could be registered. Here was a situation where the man even if he accepted and signed his paternity, could walk away from the responsibility of caring for the woman and the child. The mother had to carry the social stigma without any hope of marrying anyone. She also had the responsibility for the child. Men refused to accept paternity for various reasons. One was the loss of their standing in society.

The LTTE women went to the extent of requesting that the child be registered in the mother's name rather than the father's name. When this request was made to Pirapaharan he is supposed to have said that when Tamil Eelam was born he would be the first one to change his surname to his mother's name.

In Vanni, CWR started women's groups in villages, specifically to report on problems involving women, as a preventive measure. Since civilian women preferred to discuss their problems with married women, married members were allocated for this task. These members were given training and sent out to the villages. Invariably the married women were not as efficient as unmarried members.

Campaign Against Dowry

Jeya, later on in her role as the head of the women's political division, prepared a survey on dowry practice. Women were sent out into the society to collect data. As part of this data collection, Malaimahal wrote stories about dowry over three generations of women and how their lives had changed over generations. This was published in the SP magazine. The magazine also carried some news on the work of CWDR. None of these SP magazine issues are available today.

Sadly CWR too, never created a publication on the data that was collected on dowry. It was around this time that Adele Balasingam published her researched work on dowry, *Unbroken Chain*. All these efforts by women resulted in new laws under the LTTE that removed the word 'dowry' as illegal and introduced the notion of ungendered 'wedding gift'. Demanding a wedding gift was also made illegal.

Police and Justice Division

The LTTE police force was also formed soon after re-entering Jaffna. Pirapaharan ensured that men and women were recruited in equal numbers, not only in the police force but also in the 'Justice' section which evolved at the same time. Both the police force and the justice system continued to grow since thier formation and had been noted for the efficient delivery of service. These two bodies did not have a separate section for women but had almost 50 per cent women in it.

Those in charge of the Police division at the top were LTTE members who at that time were mostly men. But below that level women were equally represented. All the training was on par for men and women.

A woman who was one of the very first judges under the LTTE justice system summarized the courts and the police that evolved under the LTTE:

> The informal group which functioned under the name 'Justice Section' would go to the locations of conflict and investigate and resolve issues. This section was dissolved and in 1992 the Law college was started and those in the earlier informal Justice Section were taken into the Law College for training. In this too men and women were taken in equal numbers to study law. Classes were taken by older retired lawyers. The first batch of lawyers graduated in 1993.
>
> When the Justice Department was created in 1993, some of those who completed the law training were appointed as judges. There were four women and four men in the first batch of judges. We studied day and night to complete the course and also practise law. Initially we learnt the laws of Sri Lanka which in turn was based on the British law. But when we began our own courts, we had made changes to the law book to suit our country. These laws evolved over time. The laws were drafted by a group of LTTE members including our judges. Advice from outside judges were taken and their agreement was obtained. The judges of our courts were selected based on personality and preferences. Each judge was allocated to one court. Thus the four women judges were fully in charge of the courts allocated to them. Sri Lanka qualified lawyers also worked in these courts after taking oaths under the judges of Tamil Eelam.

Laws were modified so that equal rights were given to men and women. When customs and law do not agree, judges have the responsibility to make a ruling. This in turn will become law later. I was responsible for writing many new laws. I feel very sad that I have now forgotten much of what I and all the others had created. All this has been destroyed and now our minds are occupied with other things.

The name 'dowry' was banned as a legal terms and a 'gift' concept was introduced that was gender neutral. Demanding gift for marriage was punishable under the law. Divorce laws followed the common global pattern. Those who sought divorce were, however, required to undergo counselling provided by the state and also a necessary cooling off period. Religious rituals are considered legal marriage. Thus the couple are prohibited from remarrying either legally or ritually until a divorce is granted.

Domestic violence will be investigated for the cause and some efforts will be made to rectify the cause, be it drinking problems by the male or excessive nagging by the female. Once these efforts fail, divorce will be granted if sought.

Women generally have a greater work load. This gets worse if the woman also opts for outside work. In this situation this is also taken into account. Women hardly complain about their work load. They mostly come with issues of violence or because the woman's husband is having a relationship with another woman.

Parents beating children excessively is also punishable and may lead to the children being removed.

CWDR and other organizations working for the women will bring social problems that could be addressed by law.

Rape was much less compared to the rest of the island. Unlike murder which could be sometimes committed impulsively, rape is never treated like this and it is a crime for which bail is never granted. Women never bring fake cases. Earlier, rape was hidden in our society, but it was not so hidden in the LTTE society.

The man is punished for cheating a woman after promise of marriage even if there was no sexual relationship. The woman would get compensation and the man will be punished. This becomes more serious if there was a sexual relationship or if it results in a child.

There was a supreme court consisting of five judges, which is the ultimate court. It will always have a gender balance of 2:3— sometimes 3 males and sometimes 3 females. The chief judge will change from male to female each year. The same is the case for the group that was in charge of writing the laws.

Initially when students are selected for the law college they were selected from the members and thus gender balance was maintained. After the fourth batch it was all civilians who were taken into the law college. The ratio was still maintained as far as possible and there was no large imbalance.

Senior judges were in the selection committee and they also looked for the applicant's commitment to serve the people. Judges were always members.

The second batch of lawyers graduated two years later. They were also members of the LTTE. Some of the first batch lawyers were eventually promoted to be judges. Later civilians were also taken to be trained as lawyers. However, the judges in the LTTE courts were always LTTE members.

Theatre

Another movement that started in this period and flourished throughout the struggle period was theatre. It took many forms. Full length dramas that dealt with political and social issues were performed throughout the homeland on the roadside. In Tamil these are referred to as 'therukkoothtu'. This is an ancient art form that entertained ordinary people. In the past these would depict stories of kings and gods. Now they took on contemporary themes.

Women in the 'Arts and Culture' division also produced several dramas on women's issues. A Jaffna academic in the fine arts department began a group named TAG (Theatre Action Group) which also did a lot of work among the women. This was used extensively by women to alleviate trauma and discuss issues that they had difficulty talking about. This is also an area that had a deep effect on the psyche of women. The founder of TAG commenting on their early work with the LTTE women said:

> A group of LTTE women like Barathy, Kasthoori and a few others had a revolutionary aspect to their thinking. These girls liked to maintain a relationship with TAG. When one of the girls from the theatre group went to join the LTTE, the LTTE girls had sent her back saying that they admired what the TAG group was doing and that she should continue to do that. Because they were women they were more acutely aware of what needed to be done. They therefore thought beyond national liberation and about social liberation. The LTTE leader had been telling the women to do what needed to be done while he was alive. Only some of the senior men in the LTTE were supportive of what these revolutionary women wanted to achieve.

Another form of 'therukkoothtu' was staged in large open air theatres and it attempted to draw the audience into the action. It was found to be therapeutic. The TAG movement generated many other forms of action groups based on TAG techniques. The basis of these was to release their inner stresses thus enabling them to be more productive in their work, which in turn improved their stress level. Some of the workshop techniques are: create peaceful surroundings, make one feel it is a sacred place or plant some symbols that will trigger memories. Such symbols may be different for different people and it would make them cry and share their inner grief. In one such theatre, a giant scary figure was used after starting the workshop as a good peaceful place. Other times a picture was used. There would be a lot of talking to draw the audience in. Music was used extensively. Another form of theatre is indeed the 'Ponguthamil' event which was intended as an awakening process rather than a consoling workshop.

Model Village

Mithila, another SP leader, took a village, Poompohaar, and converted it into a model village. Pavana, who worked under Mithila in the early stages, worked on this model village for the improvement of the conditions in the villages. Pavana cited how by cleaning one child in a very backward village, she encouraged the mothers in the entire village to keep all their children clean. Pavana's description of this incident highlights the huge gap between the Jaffna middle class and the backward villages. When she produced a five hundred rupee note, which she had brought with her when she left home, at the tiny shop in this backward village, the shop keeper kept looking at it because he had never seen notes of such high value. Pavana said she understood the meaning of political work through this incident.

Pavana noted the unique quality of the women leaders nurtured by Thileepan. Through Mithila, Pavana learnt to think that women can do what men can do. Mithila who was disabled by war injury, still urged the women under her not to avoid hard work. Often when LTTE women took on hard tasks, the civilian women too would join in. Another training Mithila instilled in Pavana was to change the tradition and make women look straight and talk straight. They were also trained to get down to any condition and work. Even to enter private homes naturally and sit on the floor as equal to the residents and talk as equals with the women without fussing about dirt, etc.

Mithila died early due to illness.

District Heads

Women put in charge of districts had many roles including holding meetings, talking to people to join the movement, helping maaveerar families and the like. One of their roles was to visit schools and speak to the students. One could say that half the schools would welcome them and the other half reluctantly did so because they had to. The schools would also limit the time they took in the school. Women were put in charge of each Grama Sevekar division (smallest village level administrative unit). Civilian women could access them with their problems such as domestic violence, eve teasing and recruitment.

Decline of SP Activism

Santha's role in CWDR ended around 1995 with the exodus of Jaffna to Vanni. She decided to return to the battle lines and eventually left the movement in 1998, unhappy about the lack of social progress started in the earlier SP movement under Thileepan. Santha's role in the political wing of the LTTE symbolizes the evolution of women's empowerment under the LTTE. Clearly, Santha was Pirapaharan's choice of women's political leadership which was not to be. As we will see, however, this was not the end of women's development which took a different turn as the SP activism took back stage but left behind some institutional culture that persisted till the end. This together with militarism contributed to the evolution of women under LTTE from now on.

These activities, institutions and related publications like SP had started to change the conservative Jaffna society. One observation cited in one of the LTTE publications referred to a young woman at a task that would have been hard to imagine in any Tamil society. In Jaffna, farms are irrigated using water drawn from wells. A perfectly straight long trunk of a Palmyra tree is cantilevered in the middle and weighted with some large stones at one end. A long rope and bucket is tied to the other end. This permanent set up near the deep well is used to draw water from the well. When water needs are high such as for irrigating farms, a person would walk on the trunk towards the well, thus lowering the bucket into the well. Then the person will walk towards the other end of the trunk thus raising the bucket from the well. This activity was always a male domain. During this period, the north lived without electricity and women could be seen doing the same task—a visible symbol of the changes that were taking place.

The SP women, however, remained frustrated because they were unable to take up direct revolutionary action that Thileepan had taught them. The SP women, felt a lack of leadership to follow the Thileepan line of women's liberation. These frustrated women restricted their work to the divisions and related duties allocated to them. This dispersed the available energies for taking forward the women's struggle. It is possible that the decline of SP activism may have started at this point. When Jeya left her role as the head in 1995, it was taken over for short periods by Nismia and Thanikaiselvi. Owing to their very short times in this role, these two leaders could not provide the leadership to re-invigorate SP activism. By the time Thamilini took over as the head of the women's political wing in 1999, SP activism had more or less disappeared.

Another explanation given for the loss of SP activism was the loss of support Eelam Tamils had from India. India had allowed training bases for all the Eelam Tamil militant groups during 1970s and 80s. This was the cold war era when India was aligned with the Soviet Union. The dissolution of the Soviet Union and death of the Indian Prime Minister, Indira Gandhi, ended this alignment. India began aligning with the USA and began treating the Tamil struggle as problematic. Thus the isolated LTTE was compelled to take a very militaristic approach to the struggle, resulting in neglect of direct action for social revolution.

By the end of the three-year period of Indian intervention, the female members of the LTTE were mostly made up of two types—those who took training in Tamil Nadu in the first batch and those who had started their activism in SP and SOLT under Thileepan's leadership. These two groups had evolved differently and there was a clear distinction in their culture of struggle. The wave of changes and patterns of thinking that had been set by these two waves of women during the earlier phase continued to affect the society. However, soon in the years that followed militarism took the upper hand.

Caste

The strategy used, especially by the LTTE, was to ignore the caste factor in all its actions. The caste practices of Jaffna is village based and is interwoven with the trades practised by the people. Through repeated and large-scale displacements the grip, these practices had on the society, was loosened. When the entire Jaffna society relocated overnight in 1996 to Vanni, the caste system lost one of its deepest roots. In the traditional villages where the various castes were allocated their own localities, available opportunities were limited for people of different castes to interact. In the displaced places such intermingling was possible. Displacement also facilitated cross caste marriages.

The pooraali culture was unique and stood apart from the mainstream. A casteless thought was achieved in that culture. Among the pooraalis, who are fighting in the frontlines in the most trying conditions, there will invariably be a greater degree of comaraderie that furthers casteless thinking. Cross caste marriage among pooraalis was common. Crowning these changes was the Maaveerar worship of remembering their ultimate sacrifice, and practising the associated rituals without caste awareness.

The Vanni society under the LTTE existed only for about a decade. It would be foolish to say that caste was completely eradicated in that decade. The changes that have occurred and the administration where power is distributed across caste would have ensured its eradication if it were given more time. That was not to be.

Geopolitics-5

Jaffna was the centre of the evolving LTTE de facto state, from the time of the departure of the Indian forces in March 1990 until the LTTE withdrew from Jaffna to Vanni in late 1995. This chapter describes the evolution of women's action in the social space that had progressive changes for women. In this same six-year period some major milestones in the LTTE history also occurred.

The first was the eviction of one hundred thousand Muslims from the north in October 1990. The history of Muslims in the island begins with their arrival as traders 1500 years ago. They married local women and settled down and have since identified themselves with the Tamils. They have stood for elections as members of the Tamil political parties from the beginning. They actively took part in the non-violent protests of Eelam Tamils. When the armed struggle was started many Muslims joined the various armed movements in substantial numbers and have died fighting for this cause. The initial cracks in this unity began to appear during the early 1980s in the Eastern districts of Batticaloa and Amparai.

It may be enlightening to view the history of the early 1980s in Batticaloa. The British government had started to actively train Sri Lankan security forces around this time. In particular the STF unit of the police was launched with full training provided by the British and Israel military. STF immediately recruited many Muslim youth as home-guards, who were used extensively in many of the massacres of Tamils in Batticaloa and Amparai during the following decade.

These two developments must be studied together and considered for any connections. Is it possible that Britain provided the advice on how to drive a wedge between Tamils and Muslims, who have shown such solidarity for years if not millennium. The eviction of the Muslim people from Jaffna, by the LTTE is, however, a sign of the weakness of its politics which should have raised people's awareness about the plots being hatched by the powers that be. During the ceasefire period from 2002 onwards, the LTTE tried and partially succeeded to mend its relationship with the Muslim community.

Few months after the eviction of the Muslims from Jaffna in May 1991, former Indian Prime Minister Rajiv Gandhi was murdered during the election rally in Tamil Nadu, India. Within minutes of the event some in India claimed that the LTTE was behind it. The mainstream discourse continues to carry this line to this date. However, an unfinished commission of inquiry, and many books by Tamils of Tamil Nadu try to inform the public better, and the debates on the forces behind this assassination continues to this day.

The third event took place soon after in 1992. Mathaya, who had been considered the second in command in the LTTE, was removed from all his posts alleging that he was acting as an agent of RAW, the Indian intelligence. Mathaya was later executed by the LTTE.

All three events sent shock waves even among the LTTE members. The dismissal of Mathaya, who had just been appointed the overall head of the political section, would have affected a large section of the LTTE membership. The 150 women which consisted of many who were under him in Palamoddai would have been affected too. Many of the women however expressed the view of the LTTE that Mathaya was working with the Indian intelligence division.

8

Rise of Militarism: 1996-2001

The next phase in the history begins when the LTTE withdrew from Jaffna, in 1996 together with very large-scale displacement of Jaffna civilians. The LTTE set up Kilinochchi/Vanni as its main centre. The institutions described in the last chapter continued to grow in Vanni. At the same time war continued to use much of the LTTE resources including the energies of women. By the late 1990s all the women who had been groomed by Thileepan as potential leaders had either been killed, left the movement or had a taken a quiet backstage position within the movement.

A new type of women was now the leaders in the women's institutions. Many of them rose from the bottom strata of the society. Thamilini (Head of the women's political wing); Kalaimahal (Head of CWDR); Vithusha (Head of the Malathi regiment) are notable ones. This takeover was also accompanied by relatively high levels of women's employment in the LTTE institutions. The result was a highly interconnected female culture that had the ability to function in the public space. This culture, working with the existing LTTE institutions, was empowered to eliminate destitution among women.

The concurrently evolved military culture among women and their astounding success in winning many battles injected more confidence into this interconnected female culture. If the SP activism infused radicalism, the military culture created a new kind of woman who stood as inspirational models to other young civilian women. One military ex-LTTE woman, Kumi, described it thus in 2016:

It was collective action and I would think if everyone completed their task the struggle would not fail. We were always prepared to try new things that would scare many Tamil women. When we succeeded it increased our confidence.

The military roles gave us the kind of experience that ordinary civilian women never had the opportunity to face. We sometimes slept on mattresses but we also slept on the hard ground; sometimes we would just have plain rice kanji and at other times we would eat good food; we would wear good shoes but we also walked on bare feet with thorns pricking our feet; we would wear new clothes or very old clothes. We went through all kinds of experiences. We were exposed to all types of people in the society. Tamil civilian women are not exposed to the many aspects of the society. They thus lack adequate knowledge about the society. Parents protect their daughters and the daughters continue with that tendency and remain satisfied to stay within their small circle. This is almost the foundation of our society.

On the contrary, we in the movement have developed an express desire for knowing the environment. If we were in a military regiment, we would go alone just with the use of a compass for several kilometres, through forests, rough ground, rivers and settled areas. If we engaged in a battle with the enemy and became dispersed, we had to find our way back to the home base. On our reconnaissance, we may have lost the compass; even sun and the shadows may not help sometimes if it is raining heavily. In this situation, we use the landmarks like trees, shops, wells and village names which we would register as we move about. Once we do that we will be able get back using this information that we gathered as we went. Also, if we are planning an attack in a settled region like Jaffna, we would basically absorb the entire geography by roaming the place repeatedly. Indeed I am doing the same now in a new country where I have found asylum. I can see that the civilian Tamil women, who have immigrated to this country, long before I came here, are less aware of the geography in which they live. We do a similar thing when we set up up a base in the jungle. We would learn about the surroundings and the villages nearby. These experiences taught us to learn about the environment and the society more thoroughly.

Another difference between us and the civilian women is the confidence we have gained to speak out in the middle of a group of people. Civilian Tamil women also do not have a strong desire for the latest news and knowledge. They tend to restrict themselves to their children, cooking and watching television dramas. We were trained in the movement to interact more with people in the wider society. We also received the training to work according to schedule. This makes us more efficient. Our days are fully scheduled. This is a training that is missing for civilian women.

Presently in this new environment, we find it difficult to socialize with parents of our children's friends because their conversations are mundane and boring. Often civilian women have a narrow mind in acknowledging and praising the achievements of other children. Our training broadened our minds to rejoice in others' achievements. Interest in the nation and the society broadens the mind and this in turn will influence our children.

Many people around the world who have come to know Tamil women who have immigrated to these places have noticed that the ex-LTTE women often stand out from the rest of the Tamil women. People notice the difference in their demeanour and the manner in which they conduct their lives. These ex-LTTE women could be seen encouraging others who may be discouraged about something. Malar, ex-LTTE woman said:

The ex-LTTE women have experiential knowledge of facing and overcoming failures. Through experience we have gained the long-term vision to know that time has the ability to erase the hurt caused by failures.

Even the act of joining the movement gives confidence and they are told that they must develop their abilities to be doubly as good as that of the civilians.

Right from the start one has to do sentry duty at night. For young Tamil women this in itself is breaking a barrier. Guarding their camp at night with a gun helps to destroy all night fears about ghosts, snakes and insects. When women complete their basic training, which varies from three months to six months, a large part of their transformation has already taken place.

Women also increase their mental strength enormously together with their physical strength. In their homes, women are conditioned not to go out at night. This is universal among Tamil women. In contrast, the LTTE women carry out many activities at night besides sentry duty. They would take even training or clear the surroundings of their camps. In effect they do a lot of outside activities at night. Superstitious fears as well as the conditioning that women are weak and thus cannot protect themselves were both destroyed in this basic training.

Physical strength and mental confidence itself is enough to create the new woman. After the basic training, being at the battle front reinforces solidarity with fellow women. The battles placed a huge responsibility on the women's shoulders for the lives of the fellow pooraali, as well as making the struggle succeed. This was additional experiential training.

The LTTE leader would always emphasize the importance of women's participation and taking care of women's health. His attitude gave the women great strength.

Another aspect of our training was to drill us on repeated practice, to never tire of practice to succeed. Trying repeatedly was encouraged. We were also given huge responsibilities, which we would judge as beyond us. We were forced to take it on but with immense support. This was another way our confidence was boosted.

Living together in the camps naturally creates many personal confrontations. But the circumstances forced the women to not carry personal problems over long periods. Often issues were dropped quickly because they had a common goal and a common enemy. Many LTTE women have internalized this and behave like this even now in civil life.

For them, confrontations do not ruin personal relationships.

There were two high ranking roles allocated to women to deal entirely with women's issues. One is that of the head of the women's political wing and the other was what was formed around 1996 in Vanni—an overall women's group consisting of women from all the different divisions who met regularly. This second body consisting of around 20 women was called the Women's Council. What were their achievements? As one senior women stated, "Change was everyone's desire".

Makalir Peravai–Women's Council

Till 1996 there was one female head in charge of all the female divisions. Effectively this was under the commander of the women's military division. All the female divisions, military as well as political and other divisions came under her. This position was held by Jeyanthi till 1993, then Jana till 1995, then Rishana and Vithusha. All decisions went through this female head.

Around 1996 the women's sections of the LTTE underwent a major reorganization. The reorganization created separate female sections in each of the major LTTE divisions, namely: political, finance, intelligence and military. The military in turn was divided into two regiments, Sothiya and Malathi regiments with separate commanders. While the two female military heads reported directly to Pirapaharan, the heads of the three female sections of the other three divisions, mentioned above, reported to the overall heads of those respective divisions, who were invariably males.

Women poruppalar however, gathered regularly and independently even before this re-organization. It was formalized as the Makalir Peravai in 1998 because experience from 1996 to 1998 showed that important decisions regarding women in general were being taken by the female heads of various divisions without much coordination. The main goal was that general decisions concerning women were to be taken after discussion in this body to be followed by all female leaders. Eventually even civilian women's issues were considered by this body.

The Makalir Peravai had all the women poruppalar. Makalir Peravai met once a month. Pirapaharan was not present for all the meetings but was there at times. Other men were called in only as needed to investigate issues related to them and they needed to be asked questions. Many male leaders viewed this special access to the LTTE leader that the women leaders had as a privilege. Many senior male leaders of similar ranking did not have this kind of access. The members of Makalir Peravai mentioned three issues they dealt with as described below.

When the civilian girls faced harassment in lonely forest roads, a decision was made by the Makalir Peravai to give all the girls self-defence training. The women in the military division had arranged several military women to give the training throughout Vanni. Full implementation was delayed because the girls were not brought together by those who were given the tasks. Some of the women in the Makalir Peravai faulted Thamilini who was given this responsibility, for failing to do this.

Makalir Peravai also decided that saris should not be made compulsory for civilian women working in the LTTE institutions. Pirapaharan had told Thamilini to initiate the change by talking to the women and the poruppalar of the various divisions. Pirapaharan believed changes to long held societal practices should not be made by strict orders. Thus Thamilini was asked to work towards the change. Some fault Thamilini for not being proactive in this regard.

After marriage, the women LTTE tended to lower their priority for work outside the home. Their husbands tended to prefer the women to remain as housewives. Married women also tended to think that the home was enough. The women's section had difficulty in convincing the women to come back and continue her work outside home. More than half the married women showed reluctance to return to work. The women's section supported the women to come out against their husband's wishes but some women did not show this determination. One can see the effect of the loss of SP activism at the expense of militarism at work in this attitude of the married LTTE women.

Classes by SP Women

One of the SP women Nila stated:

> I was injured in battle and from 1995 I worked again on women's projects. Later I took classes to the LTTE women. I also did a lot of translation work. I translated a whole book about Britain's Special Air Service men's (SAS) war stories. I had held classes about the Nicaraguan struggle and the Stalingrad battle which was a battle from building to building. I gave classes about it because it is a good example for us for the Jaffna battle.

A division called 'Kalvi kuzhu' came directly under the overall political head. Its responsibilities included pooraali education. This was run in two streams: general politics for pooraalis and English language.

Desire for Battles

Women who were working in the political division and thus with the civilian women often cite the prevailing prestige given to military roles and the work in the political division being regarded as inferior. One woman said that even though she found working among civilian women exhilarating, she still desired military roles because of the prevailing attitudes. Women have fasted demanding that they be sent to the battle lines.

At a later stage, there was another reason for the lower opinion of political work which was euphemistically referred as 'parappurai' (propaganda). Till the displacement from Jaffna in 1995, the LTTE was very selective in who they recruited. It had turned away people who wanted to join. However, once in Vanni, due to many military battles and fewer available people, the LTTE was compelled to go on recruitment drives through 'parappurai'. The 'parappurai' responsibility was tasked to the political division. Thus the same women who worked with the civilian women were now also expected to do the recruitment 'parappurai'. This made people suspicious and it became problematic to work with the civilian women.

As new women joined later, the SP leaders were sidelined as not suitable for the military focused struggle in Vanni. One SP woman said:

> The SP women continued to demand that they should maintain the independence of women while the new ones wanted to run with the men and act like men. Thileepan's pupils were straight talkers and uncompromising implementers who refused to go along with compromises and demand equal resources for the women.

One SP women described one of the efforts she was part of in Vanni in 1999 with a lot of frustration:

> Many women leaders came together to implement a project in a selected village. The medium we used was drama and music. Most of us in this project were influenced by Thileepan.
>
> We started at the school level and then reached out to the village, all through drama. It was entertainment as well as encouraging communication and leadership. It was progressing well. The village was brought out to the school grounds and the work progressed. The project raised the awareness among the people. The whole village was ready to stand behind the leaders of the project. But it all came to a sudden end. Women involved in the project were transferred out of the political division. I suspect it was because it was not military focused.

The Beginnings of the Female Land Black Tiger Unit

The rise of militarism and the related desire to take part in battles is exemplified in this piece of writing in the publication, *Viluthaaki Veerumaaki*, which records the history of the Malathi

Regiment. It describes how women demanded to become land black tigers. There have already been women sea black tigers (translated by the author):

> Many of the female pooraalis, who had been active in the battle fronts for a long time, had begun to see the importance of a female land black tiger unit. Their battle front experience had taught them that in difficult battle situations, two black tigers can achieve the level of destruction that can otherwise be achieved only by a large regiment. Captain Miller had done this in 1987 on a Lankan unit stationed in Nelliyadi. In 1990 Lt. Col. Borg removed hurdles during the battle to destroy the Mankulam Lankan military camp. The following year, during the attack to destroy the Mannar-Silavathurai Lankan military camp, Major Dambo became a legend. After a two-year gap, black tigers had entered the Palali Lankan military camp and carried out substantive destruction.
>
> In the sea, attacks by the sea black tigers unit were expanding. Beginning with Major Kantharooban, Capt. Vinoth and Capt. Colins, their extraordinary history had continued with Capt. Angkayatkanni, Lt. Col. Nalayini and Major Mankai. It would not be an exaggeration to say that the boat service between Jaffna and the Vanni mainland through the Kilali strait was possible during that time only with the strength of the sea black tiger unit.
>
> Female sea black tigers like, Lt. Col. Nalayini, Major Mankai, Major Mathusha and Major Rosha left the female land units and joined the female sea tiger units. This trend to desire to become black tigers continued. Many female pooraalis in land units continued to inform through letters to Thalaivar of their desire to become black tigers. They had received replies from Thalaivar that their request had been accepted and they would be called when the need arose. Such letters kept arriving at the Thalaivar's place. Many who expressed such a wish and were waiting to become black tigers had become maaveerar in other battles.
>
> It was early 1996. The Suriyakathir-02 operation was yet to begin. Malathi regiment commander Vithusha brought a

message from Thalaivar. She brought together everyone who had expressed the wish to become a black tiger and gave them the message from Thalaivar. The message was that before becoming a black tiger they must train in reconnaissance missions.

It was after this, black tigers like Capt. Inthu and Major Srivaani joined the reconnaissance team lead by Maithily. Their work in this team, which started in the relatively battle free period prior to Suruyakathir-02, continued through the Elephant-pass battle, Mullaitheevu battle and on to reconnaissance work during Victory-assured-01, 02 and 03 operations. They performed with excellence during these dangerous and unexpected situations.

By now, all the regiments in the Malathi Division had gone to Mullaitheevu for training for the next battle. The black tigers who had received their training in the reconnaissance unit had again informed Thalaivar of their desire and readiness for action.

The reply said, 'Please wait'. Vithusha took the black tigers away from battle duties and made them stay in one of our administrative base in Katsilaimadu.

The hours turned into days. They waited for their call each day. No call came. The days became weeks. But still no call came.

Twice female black tiger units had been formed and training had been given. But due to shortages of human resource they were given other duties. Thus to ensure that their numbers were not reduced this time, Vithusha had resisted involving them in other tasks. Ever since the Suriyakathir-02 operation, only one or two people with insufficient reconnaissance experience had been put into such work in the Mullaitheevu battle.

The waiting black tigers started to feel frustrated just sitting around in the administrative base with neither the battle duties nor the training for black tigers. Vithusha at this time was spending most of her time in Mullaitheevu where her units were training. It was difficult to get a meeting with her. The black tigers came to a decision. Suki who was with the administrative part of the camp recalled the event thus:

> The sadness of pooraalis departure from us is always there even though we accept that their departure is for a greater goal. We knew that the black tigers' days with us were numbered. We were thus looking after them with special care as best as we could. That day those who took tea for them in the morning returned with the tea saying that they refused to take the tea.

All the others who were at that camp were leaders in charge of administration for the various units. The leaders asked the black tigers to take the tea but they refused. The leaders promised them that they would ask Vithusha to talk to Thalaivar about their wishes. The black tigers remained adamant.

They refused breakfast too. Others did not eat either. Black tigers meant more to us than the others who trained together, fought together and were injured. When those who were about to go as black tigers refused food who can eat?

When Vithusha heard that they were on a fast that whole day, she arrived late that night. She pacified them saying she would speak to Thalaivar about sending them for training soon. At last the black tigers agreed to eat. She informed Thalaivar of their determination.

Thalaivar arrived with Gadafi to see them. This is how Gadafi recalled that meeting:

> Vithusha had informed Thalaivar that there are thirty women waiting to get black tiger training. Thalaivar had promised to see them immediately but other work had delayed the meeting. That day I went with him to see them. Thalaivar promised to take them into training immediately. Within a few days of that meeting we had taken them in for training.

Maithily who was badly injured in the Sooriyakathir Operation-02 was made the leader of that black tiger unit. Vithusha selected some female pooraalis to run the administrative side of the black tiger unit. Vithusha bid farewell to the unit on its way to black tiger training. The black tigers who fasted to become black tigers went for the training delighted. Thus the female land black tiger unit began functioning as an independent unit under the leadership of Maithily.

Militarism vs Social Revolution

The launch of armed struggle among Eelam Tamils and in particular the active participation of women in the struggle was focused on revolutionary social changes. Historically, Thileepan is seen as the one who took this to great heights by attracting women into the struggle.

Yet, throughout this work the attraction of military pursuits among the pooraalis has been highlighted. Military success in defeating the 'enemy' had a therapeutic effect on a people who had been subjected to decades of state-sponsored pogroms. Prior to the Indian intervention, militarism though attractive for this reason, was still moderated by the need for social revolution.

After the war with the Indian forces, due to the loss of back stage support in Tamil Nadu, militarism became the only option for the struggle to succeed. The LTTE was now forced to devote less of its resources to the earlier focus on revolutionary social changes. To the outsider, the LTTE now started to appear as a purely military outfit. The women's narratives show the tension. As one woman said, "change was in everyone's mind...", but battles were draining their resources.

The importance of military battles to keep the homeland regions under the control of the Tamils was clearly demonstrated in the post-2009 phase. The burning land issues, the presence of the military in "peace time", erection of Buddha statues in Tamil areas where there are no Buddhists are a clear demonstration of the need for Tamils to control the Tamil land. It shows why militarism was the precondition needed to keep the social revolution moving.

9

Women's Development in Southern Tamil Eelam

As depicted in the chart in Chapter 3, this work is incomplete regarding the developments of women in southern Tamil Eelam. In this chapter a very brief outline of the developments in this part of Tamil Eelam is described. The developments in southern Tamil Eelam took a very different route to the northern parts due to demographic differences. Though armed struggle probably started in Batticaloa and Trincomalee much earlier than in the north, they were later absorbed into the movements that arrived from the north. One name frequently mentioned in this regard is an armed movement called 'Nagar Padai' that evolved very early in Batticaloa. This early development of armed struggle in southern Tamil Eelam has not been documented. It is clear that these early movements did not attract women. Indeed one Batticaloa resident said that even during the earlier non-violent struggle led by the Federal Party, women of southern Tamil Eelam did not partake.

During the 1980s, northern-based armed groups, other than the LTTE, had been established in southern Tamil Eelam. Men from this region had joined these groups in very large numbers, probably even in greater numbers than Jaffna. Women from the south had some participation in these groups. However, the society did not condone this because it was seen as indiscipline. The PLOTE was one of the early armed groups that became very active. Later many, who were in the PLOTE, joined the LTTE. The EPRLF also started functioning in Batticaloa earlier than the LTTE. They had created many civilian bodies for the different sectors such as: women, farmers, fishermen, etc. They set up women's bodies in every village. Another armed group, Tamil Makkal Pathukaappu Peravai, was also popular during the 1980s, which operated throughout the Tamil Eelam region as well as among the upcountry Tamils. It had carried out the very first guerrilla attack in Batticaloa.

LTTE began operating in Batticaloa much later, only in 1986. The LTTE student body was established after this. This body coordinated the protests and enforced discipline among students. The student body's main focus, however, was improving the education of children and not much was done regarding political education. There was no parallel student uprising like what took place in Jaffna. Though a handful of women had joined earlier, larger numbers joined the armed movement during the Indian intervention.

The first batch training in Batticaloa for women took place after this for fire or six women. Among them was the first female maaveerar from southern Tamil Eelam, Anitha. Anitha is remembered for her political work among both Tamil and Muslim communities in south Tamil Eelam. For this work she had to move through Indian military controlled areas while travelling between Batticaloa and Amparai districts. Her movements were leaked to the Indian military and she was captured in 1988. She took her life by biting cyanide to avoid being in custody.

One of the senior women from Trincomalee who had joined in 1990 did so only after displacing Vanni following military operations. She said:

> In Trincomalee, the LTTE members did not move out during the daytime and would come to our area only during the night. Even then I have not seen women fighters during those days. I, however, remember some women leaving Trincomalee to join the movement. The earliest ones took training in 1988. Even after this, those women who joined would be sent to Vanni for training. I have never seen women with arms around my

village. It was assumed that those carrying arms are always men. The LTTE did not administer a region like they did in the north. This was the main reason women did not join. If they did, the Sinhala military would come and take the family members away. Women had better protection in the LTTE administered regions in the north. The southern Tamil Eelam region was still in the guerrilla war stage.

Most of the women who joined from Trincomalee were from areas like Moothoor. They were from extremely poor families. They had very little education. Educated women from Trincomalee rarely joined. One reason could be that the members were hardly visible and always operated secretively. Even the inhabited areas that were supposedly in the control of the LTTE were different to what it was like in the north. There were no sentry points and demarcated areas.

The very first group of women fighters went to Trinco only in 1999. One woman from this group commented:

> For example, people in the village of Pattalipuram in Trincomalee were extremely poor. Children as young as four would be left alone to go to town and beg. Adults would either go hunting, collecting fire wood or collecting honey. There were no schools for eight kilometres. Their homes would be just four poles with a sari over it. Places like these were the ones that were mostly in the control of the LTTE. Even this was only after 2000.

This narrative on the participation of women from southern Tamil Eelam is also substantiated by the maaveerar statistics presented in the Table below based on the statistics published by the LTTE in July 2008. This shows a very low number of women on a per capita basis recruited into the LTTE from southern Tamil Eelam. This is even more striking given that the maaveerar statistics of males from southern Tamil Eelam is as high as the highest region in the north.

Another explanation put forward by an ex-LTTE member from Batticaloa is as follows:

Women from the north were more eager to join the struggle because they also saw it as a path to eradicate the curse of dowry-giving practice. This is absent in the southern region. People donate land to the newly married to farm that land but this is never part of a marriage bargain. Also caste practice was milder in the south. Thus the drive to struggle against this was less. Some LTTE members from Batticaloa who went to Jaffna may have been treated like untouchables by the northern civilians. Later, during the split by Karuna, he used this accusation to good effect to support his actions. Another cause for the difference in caste practice derives from differing religious practices. Most people in the south worshipped the female goddess Amman, who according to ancient Tamil literature is the god of coastal areas. Older temples in Batticaloa had local non-Brahmin priests. Some of the Jaffna habits, however, were later imported to the south.

Civilian Women of the South

During the early 1990s and late 1990s many older women were part of a group called 'Mothers' Front' who protested against the atrocities of both the Sri Lankan and Indian military in Tamil Eelam. In an article that appeared in a 2005 issue of *Viduthalai Pulikal,* the official LTTE publication, a senior woman LTTE member describes how some of these older women had supported the armed struggle and the pooraalis. One such woman, Pooranam Amma was from Arayampathi in Batticaloa. She fed almost every pooraali in the region with her small income from sewing. Her only son was also a maaveerar.

Eelam Tamils also celebrate another such woman, Poopathi Amma from Batticaloa who was part of the Batticaloa Mothers' Front. She fasted to death during the time of the Indian intervention demanding that the Indian government implement a ceasefire and start negotiations with the LTTE. Her fast to death followed immediately after Thileepan's fast to death in 1987.

Pakkiam Amma is one such older woman from Jaffna about whom the well-known LTTE writer/maaveerar, Kasthoori, had written a moving short story. Pakkiam Amma persisted in helping the LTTE pooraalis, when much of the society shunned them due to fear of the Indian forces. She was eventually brutally killed by paramilitary forces that were working with the Indian forces.

What is Revealed in the Maaveerar Statistics of 2008

The Table shows the official release of the Maaveerar statistics as at July 2008. Note that the district indicated is the birthplace of the Maaveerar and not the location where he/she was martyred. It is reasonable to assume that this is also proportionally represented in the pooraali statistics for the districts.

The data in the Table is summarized in the smaller Table for the three regions, namely, Jaffna, Larger Vanni and the East. The 1981 census data for Eelam Tamils have also been added for these three areas. This summary Table reveals the follows points:

1. On a per capita basis Vanni districts have given the highest number to the struggle both among males and females. Given that this is where the LTTE fought its biggest battles this is not surprising.

2. The male Maaveerar from southern Tamil Eelam is comparable to the Vanni districts. This is very impressive given that the LTTE hardly administered a region in southern Tamil Eelam.

3. The female statistics from the southern region of Tamil Eelam are a surprise for many people. This may in fact be because the LTTE hardly administered a region here.

Shoba of EPRLF. The first female Maaveerar of Tamil Eelam Struggle

Malathi. The first female Maaveerar of the LTTE

Anitha. The first female Maaveerar of South Tamil Eelam

Black Tiger

Many Firsts

Official Maaveerar Statistics of August 2008

Year	Jaffna		Batti/Am-parai		Vanni		Trinco		Mul-laitheevu		Mannar		Outside		Total		All total
	M	F	M	F	M	F	M	F	M	F	M	F	M	F	M	F	
1982	1														1		1
1983	11						4								15		15
1984	20		7		3		8		6		6				50		50
1985	46		60		14		41		8		14		5		188		188
1986	91		94		20		48		21		36		9	1	319	1	320
1987	247	5	76		46	3	55		17	1	48	5	15		504	14	518
1988	127	7	114	1	39	1	39		18	1	18	1	16		371	11	382
1989	147	2	86		56		47		37		27		18		418	2	420
1990	277	41	181	4	140	11	124	2	74	11	64	1	33	2	893	72	965
1991	511	104	312	19	180	33	173	18	114	19	101	15	22	1	1413	209	1622
1992	224	45	243	9	83	6	67	1	40	7	48	6	13		718	74	792
1993	215	49	280	18	110	28	78	6	55	11	61	12	5		804	124	928
1994	90	11	162		30		42		18	1	22		2		366	12	378
1995	420	177	433	15	150	43	83	6	60	25	64	19	10	3	1220	288	1508
1996	448	142	320	33	129	53	85	13	54	26	55	14	4	4	1095	285	1380
1997	522	227	643	65	168	92	120	19	91	52	46	44	15	8	1605	507	2112
1998	364	270	429	94	134	141	102	36	58	69	54	22	17	16	1158	648	1806
1999	362	203	323	71	144	118	80	19	86	57	51	23	7	5	1053	496	1549
2000	475	318	228	79	234	179	100	27	106	78	62	45	35	17	1240	743	1983
2001	171	117	122	28	74	58	45	12	41	27	31	22	8	6	492	270	762
2002	11	5	5	5	6	1	6		2	3		1		1	30	16	46
2003	31	5	10	1	6	2	6	1	4	1	3	1	1		61	11	72
2004	9	4	41	10	5	1	5		3	2	0	0	0	0	63	17	80
2005	9	4	20	10			11		1	1	1				42	15	57
2006	170	111	178	13	130	81	174	24	40	19	35	9	20	2	747	259	1006
2007	332	62	170	10	248	42	69	5	147	28	52	12	19		1037	159	1196
2008	284	142	49	5	278	151	56	11	181	80	51	29	6		905	418	1323
Total	5615	2051	4586	490	2427	1044	1668	200	1282	519	950	281	280	66	16808	4651	21459
Total	7666		5076		3471		1868		1801		1231		346		21459		

Summary of Maaveerar Statistics By Geographic Region

	census 1981	Maaveerar total	I in population who is maaveerar	Male maaveerar	in Male popula- 1 tion who is a maaveerar	Female maaveerar	in Female 1 population who is a maaveerar	female among % maaveerar
South TE	410000	6944	(17%) 59	6254	(30%) 33	690	(3%) 297	11
L.Vanni	302000	6503	(21%) 46	4659	(31%) 32	1844	(12%) 81	40
Jaffna	700000	7666	(11%) 91	5615	(16%) 62	2051	(6%) 170	27
Total	1410000	21458	(15%) 65	16808	(23%) 42	4651	(7%) 151	21

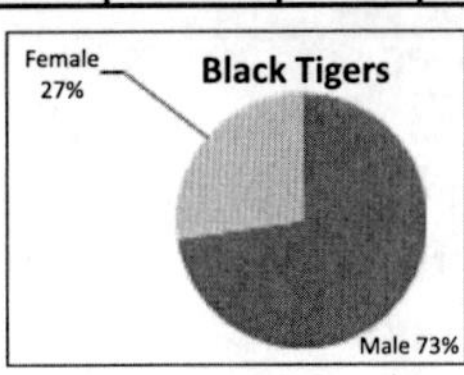

TABLE-2 Black Tigers

	Male	Female	Total	F%
Land	82	21	103	19
Sea	180	77	257	30
Total	262	98	360	27

10

Pre-2009 Women's Writing

The history that this work attempts to document is mainly based on the narratives of women who were involved in the armed struggle. It will be of some value at this point to bring to the notice of the readers the substantial volume of writing by women, who were involved in the armed struggle. A larger compilation of some of their notable works, translated, is available on the web[27]. A bibliography of the works by women can be found at the end of this chapter. Most of the writers mentioned in this bibliography are no more. This work by the women complements this history project. This chapter lists a few brief extracts from this body of writing by two well-known LTTE women writers.

The first writer listed is Barathy who has already been mentioned several times in this book. She was killed in 1993. Therefore her role in the armed movement was short. She was active in the student movement SOLT and took military training during the presence of the Indian military. These are some verses from her poem about the UN titled 'Oh the UN'

> The tall buildings of the UN
> Stands strong and high
> On the strength of human bones
> Its colourful flags flutter - like
> Countless lives it swallowed
> ...
> The hen protects its young
> But you protect the vultures
> Bloated with lives of the poor

The vultures belly peaks out
Unable to hide under your wings

In another poem 'Rise Up for the New Dawn' Barathy writes:

The land is silent
Grieving for her young daughter
Crushed trees, wingless birds
And the burning bushes
Stand up straight with their injuries
Their marks of freedom struggle.

On the soil muddied by blood
Our feet speed towards the goal
Memory-filled eyes await
The next dawn.

Malaimahal was a prolific writer who lived and wrote till the end. Her fate at the end of the war in 2009 remains unknown. In one of her non-fiction writings in 1999, titled 'My Doors are Open...' she writes about the kinder type of male chauvinism:

> I sense that over the generations my intelligence and competence are being denied. I have always been capable of achieving anything to which I put my mind. I have always had the leadership capabilities to manage large enterprises. Yet, what I see the large numbers in front me, are people who refuse to meet my intelligence with theirs but who try to control me with the power given to them. The greatest regret I have is that it is so hard to find people who are willing to respect my intelligence and competence and understand my feelings. Ever since the matriarchal societies were destroyed, I have been searching for such good people. I am yet to meet them.
>
> The people I see either want to control me with their power or try to restrict me with their protective love. When neither succeeds they call me 'uncontrollable' or 'strange' and they throw criticisms at me to blunt me. For a long time they had this longing that I should be at least a step below them. They could never acknowledge in front of others that I have

> wisdom. They are greatly satisfied when they are able to show them off as wise in front of people while I remain silent and pretend ignorance. When by some chance it is revealed that women are capable, the outrage they show is astounding. At such times if they could they would kill me. How can I shake hands with them?

In another one titled 'New Stories of Our Time', Malaimahal strings together a few milestones in the history of women's participation in the armed struggle. These milestones she uses are separated in time by several years. She uses it to highlight a new awakening among the people. The milestones Malaimahal uses are:

The Adampan battle in October 1986, which was the very first battle in which female pooraalis took an active role;

Malathi was the first female pooraali to die in battle on October 27, 1987.

Sea Tiger women wearing shorts and swimming was breaking the taboo of the time.

Angkayatkanni was a female Black Sea Tiger who died in action.

Malaimahal uses these events and writes:

> Those gathered in front of the house for 'the conference' found it difficult to believe.
>
> "Do you think these women would have really shot at the Indian military?"
>
> Though they had already heard of the Adampan battle where women had taken an active role, the battle in which Lt. Col. Victor was killed, those at 'the conference' were still not ready to believe it. With this question the conference was launched.
>
> ...
>
> 'The conference' participants who were earlier surprised had now reached a natural state of mind.
>
> Suddenly the father of the house heard noises coming from inside the House—the sound of a stick beating on the floor. He stood up shocked. Is that little boy trying to kill some small insect? The older girl who was studying is going to be

frightened. He ran inside and let out a cry of fear at what he saw. His daughter was carrying a half dead snake on a stick.

"Bring some kerosene. Let us burn this."

While it must be said that the majority of the LTTE women did not express such insights into the global pretence as in the poem about the UN by Barathy or about the societal treatment of females, as expressed by Malaimahal, many of the women did. The rise of militarism tended to diminish the open expression of these but they were there lying dormant.

In another story, *Ethuvarai,* she brings out the fun and frolicking that was common among pooraalis both female and male. She writes:

> Everyone was busy working to shift the front line security posts further to the front. These are loud mouthed women even in ordinary times. That day the noise and the frolicking had increased many fold. The fence made of Palmyra leaves was growing high by the minute. They were running to the Palmyra groove nearby to cut young leaves and were using it to make the fence. They did not bother to flatten the leaves first with their feet. Surely, the military is not going to wait for us to take the time to flatten the leaves. There was no rule as such on about what material can be used to raise the fence. Whatever they could lay their hands on went on the fence. The raincoats that the military had discarded during the Unceasing Waves-02 operation, the corrugated iron sheets bent by falling artillery which were then flattened by our 'delicate' fingers—all these became material for the fence. To tie them together, broken cables, strips of sarongs, and shoe-laces recovered from shoes discarded by the military were being used. Together with this material these active birds were building the fence at great speed.
>
> When someone ordered, 'Hey the sound is getting too much. Be quiet. He is going to fire a shell', the noise level will go down and then gradually it will rise again. An experienced person reprimanded them for their irresponsible conduct.
>
> A younger one retorted back, 'Why do you keep grumbling like a ripping cloth'?
>
> 'Don't talk like an idiot. You will know when a shell

explodes on your head', came the reply.

Another one dropped the work she was doing and lay down on the heap of soil created by those digging the trench. With her legs crossed she suggested seriously, 'All right. We are tired. Bring those meat rolls and tomato sauce. We will work after we have eaten.'

The one standing near kicked her and said very irritated, 'Why the hell are you reminding us what is not there?'

The one, who was in the trench digging, dropped her spade and climbed out saying, 'Wait. I will put this one in the trench and cover her.' She tried to roll her into the trench.

The one lying down twisted herself so that she landed in the trench standing up and immediately climbed out and made faces at the one who pushed her. A great chase followed.

Everyone dropped their work and cheered the two who were chasing.

Kasthoori

Vaanathi

Malaimahal

Popular LTTE Women Writers

Feminist Street Drama

Bibliography

This is a bibliography of all known published works by Eelam Tamil women who had carried arms during the armed struggle and the writings of Eelam Tamil women who had first-hand experience living and working with the Tamil women who were carrying arms. A good collection of such past publications have been archived at the Padippakam and Noolaham archive sites. These are listed in eight different categories below.

Works by Tamil Tiger Women

There is a vast collection of publications by both the Tamil Tigers as well the Women's Division of the Tamil Tigers that contains writings of the Tamil Tiger women. Some of which are:

1. *Suthanthira Paravaikal,* Women's Division of the Tamil Tigers. This is the foremost collection of publications issued regularly that contains mainly the writings of the Tamil Tiger women. Currently, except for a few issues, these appear to be unavailable.
2. *Naattru,* Women's Research Centre of the Tamil Tigers—a regular issue that also appears to be unavailable.
3. *Velichcham,* Arts and Culture Division of the Tamil Tigers, a regular issue.
4. *Erimalai,* International Branch of the Tamil Tigers, a regular issue.
5. *Vaanathiyin Kavithaikal*—Poetry Collection, Vaanathy, Publication Division, Tamil Tigers, 1991.
6. *Kasthooriyin Aakkankal*—Writings, Kasthoori, Publications Division, Tamil Tigers, 1992
7. *Kaathoodu Sollividu*—Writings, Barathy, Publication Division, Women's Division of the Tamil Tigers, 1993
8. *Eluthaatha un Kavithai*—Poetry Collection by Various Women, Capt. Vaanathi Publications, Women's Division of the Tamil Tigers, 2001.

9. *Viluthaaki Veerumaaki*—History of the Second Lt. Malathi Regiment, authors: A. Kantha, S. Puradchikaa and Malaimahal, Second Lt. Malathi Regiment Publications, 2003.
10. *Malaimahal Kathaikal*—Short Story Collection, Malaimahal, Capt. Vaanathi Publications, Women's Division of the Tamil Tigers, 2004.
11. *Meendum Thulirkkum Vasantham*—Poetry Collection, Ampuli, Capt. Vaanathi Publications, Women's Division of the Tamil Tigers, 2004.
12. *Vali*—Short Story Collection, Capt. Vaanathi Publications, Tamil Tiger Women's Division, 2005.
13. *Pooraaliyin Kaathali*—Novella Based on the Pre-2009 Period, Vettichelvi, Cholan Padaippakam, Tamil Nadu, 2012.

Adele Balasingam's Writings

Based on the qualification that this bibliography is of writings by Tamil women, Adele Balasingam will not qualify. However, she occupies a special place because her book on LTTE women remains to date the only authentic writing in English about LTTE women. This work, however, only describes the military achievements of the LTTE women.

Women Fighters of Liberation Tigers, Adele Balasingam, Tamil Tigers, 1993.

Work by Women Who Opposed the War

1. *Sollaatha Seithikal*, Collection of Poetry by Many Civilian Anti-War Women, 1986.

End of the War Experience

1. *Eelap Poorin Iruthi Naatkal*—First-Hand Experience of the End of the War, Vettichelvi, Cholan Padaippakam, Tamil Nadu, 2012
2. *Oolikkaalam*—Novel Based on First-Hand Experience of the End of the War, Thamilkavi, Thamilini Publishers,

Tamil Nadu, 2013.

3. *A Fleeting Moment in My* ...—First-Hand Experience of Last Years, N. Malathy, Clarity Press, USA, 2012.
4. *Enathu Naatil Oru Thuli Neeram*—The above in Tamil Translation, Vidiyal Publishers, Tamil Nadu, 2013.

Post 2009 Publications of Much Earlier Experience

1. *Tamil Tigress*—Author's experience of less than one year (88-1987) membership in the Tamil Tiger movement, Niromi de Souyza, Allen & Unwin, 2011. Though touted as memoirs there is evidence that many of the sections in the book are fictitious.
2. *Ahaalam*—1970s Experience of Activism and Torture, Pushparanee, Karuppu Pirathikal, 2013.
3. *Oru Koor Vaalin Nilali*—Memoir of the Ex-Leader of the Women's Section of the Political Wing of the LTTE, Thamilini, Kalachuvadu Pathippakam, 2016. Writing this memoir living in Colombo, Thamilini's narrative twisted the truth according to several many others who were with her in many of the incidents she describes.

Post 2009 Experience of LTTE Women

1. *Kaanaamal Poonavanin Manaivi*—Short Story Collection, Vettichelvi, Cholan Padaippakam, 2012.
2. *Ummath*—Novel based only on post-2009 experience with Tamil Tiger women, Sarmila Seiyith, Kalachuvadu Publishers, 2013. The author does not describe any experience with arms carrying women.
3. *Aarippoona Kayankalin Vali*—Vettichelvi, 2016.

11

During the Peace Process 2002-2006

The Norwegian brokered ceasefire between the LTTE and the Sri Lankan government was signed in February 2002. This was the result of the LTTE gaining military parity with the Sri Lankan government which was achieved by giving priority to militarism as we saw in the previous chapters. At the time of this ceasefire, the LTTE civil administrative structures were operating from the Vanni region with Kilinochchi as its main centre. The LTTE had been developing its de facto state structures in the Vanni for just over five years. These de facto state structures continued to grow and develop over the ceasefire period of a further five years. This structure is shown in Appendix-3.

The development of women during this phase can be appreciated with this background. The end result of a mixture of the earlier SP activism and the later militarism had a remarkable effect on the status of women in the society under the LTTE. Very few women in this society openly talked about feminism as understood in the discourse of the Western feminism which began around the 1970s. Rather, what existed in Vanni was a connected female culture which could be described as a female civil society.

Tamils living outside the LTTE administered society envisaged a liberated military LTTE woman because that is the image that the LTTE portrayed through its media. The more fundamental changes that had taken place within have not been appreciated. What was appreciated were the readily visible features. The military training had improved the women's demeanour that was otherwise conditioned by a culture that demanded a strictly subordinate role. Participation in battles raised their status to that of the LTTE men in the eyes of the general population. The LTTE membership also gave these women the freedom to act in the public space in ways that were not acceptable for the civilian women. LTTE women were clearly different from the rest of the women.

In the civilian space too there were some visible features. More women were on the streets during peak hours dressed for work, indicating a greater percentage of women in Vanni who went to work outside the home. There were also more women in civilian clothes riding motorbikes on Vanni roads compared to the rest of the island. Women occupied the public space in large numbers. They were very visible on the roads and in the LTTE institutions. This gave Vanni a uniquely pro-woman character, which was absent elsewhere on the island.

All the institutions that were set up under Jeya during 1990-1995 existed in this period too. Some have grown to be very vibrant while others had become low key. The CWDR had expanded to include many sub-institutions to cater for the needy women. CWR while being lower key was publishing a magazine called *Naattru* (Seedling) which carried many pro-women articles. The LTTE police force and its associated courts, made up mostly of civilians, had near 50 per cent female representation. This was quite an achievement. Even the laws enacted by the LTTE to be implemented by its courts had a gender equality that was absent in the Lankan laws. Lankan laws had remnants of older customary laws of the land. Indeed LTTE laws had some unique features that went overboard to protect women who may have been cheated by men with the promise of marriage.

LTTE women, women employed by the LTTE institutions, and self-employed women were all interconnected through the many LTTE institutions, resulting in this unique female culture. These women openly and routinely discussed domestic violence and other problems faced by women. They were all on the look out for women who needed a helping hand. Several of the LTTE institutions like those related to health, welfare, banking, development, police, law, and media, supported this female culture by providing supporting services. Many of these institutions had more than 50 per cent female representation. Some of them were run solely by women, both LTTE women and civilian women. Women needing help were directed to the appropriate institutions, which were all focused on giving a helping hand to women. This was the best feature of this female culture—the elimination of destitution through universal women's action. It was a unique kind of feminism, created by connecting the majority of women living all over Vanni, from all walks of life, for public action regarding women and children in need of help.

The women who were in the LTTE had joined the movement for a multitude of reasons which included: a desire to take revenge for killing their loved ones; to avoid becoming victims of sexual abuse and instead have a sense of empowerment; displacement and the destruction of the existing institutions and life as IDPs; other senior female members acting as role models; poverty and inability to go to school due to the poverty; the LTTE's nationalistic campaigns and lastly family abuse.

Between male and female members a degree of separation was maintained within the LTTE. They did come together for executing specific tasks, both in civilian and military spheres. Two opposing views on whether this separation assisted or hindered women's development prevailed in Vanni. On the one hand was the view that it permitted freer development of women. The implementation of discipline was also seen as better when it was carried out in segregated spaces. On the other hand was the view that women lost out on exposure to male-dominated knowledge and skills because of too much separation. In Vanni the tension between these two views was being gradually resolved as men and women came together increasingly to do tasks in many spheres. The majority of the female members within LTTE reported directly to female leaders. This hierarchy was intercepted somewhere up the chain by a male leader. In the case of military divisions, the interception by a male leader would only be at the very top, Pirapaharan himself. Within the political division of the LTTE, there was a separate women's section with a female leader. All female members within the political division of the LTTE eventually reported to this female leader up the hierarchy. She in turn reported to the leader of the political division, invariably a male, who in turn reported to the LTTE leader, Pirapaharan. However, the Makalir Peravai, the parallel group made up of female leaders, was a key body that handled women's issues.

Despite the impressive achievements, there was stagnation in the efforts to take this process forward during this period. Several factors contributed to this stagnation. The focus on the peace process and the attention diverted to the huge numbers of VIP visitors who arrived in Vanni, the 2004 tsunami and the ensuing political fallouts of denying aid reaching the LTTE regions, the premature and sudden dissolution of parliament, the focus on war which followed contributed to the diversion.

The one woman LTTE leader who had the responsibility to take up women's issues at this time was Thamilini, who was the head of the women's section of the political division. This all important position charged with the responsibility to undertake the development of women had been held by about five women since its inception in 1990. The very first head of the women's political division, Jeya, held the post for almost five years. Over the next four years, two women held the post for very short periods. In 1999 Thamilini took up this post and remained so till the end in 2009 with six months break over 2007-08. Thus she is by far the most important person, since the death of Thileepan and the SP activism, charged with the responsibility of improving the women's lot under the LTTE.

Connected Female Space

When Thamilini joined the LTTE she was assigned to Jeya and thus Thamilini too was influenced by Jeya's style of leadership that lacked the background of SP activism. If one is to look for efforts made to improve the women's lot under the LTTE during the last ten years prior to 2009, one must look at the achievements of Thamilini. To her credit, she has excellent oratory skills. She held political classes for the new recruits which were described by other women as excellent. These skills also made her an excellent person for recruitment. Coming from the downtrodden strata of society and rising to this level in the LTTE, her heart was also with the downtrodden. Women also describe two tendencies in Thamilini which may have been hurdles in her efforts for the development of women. She was unable to develop a good working relationship with women who were senior to her in age and years of time in the LTTE. This would have led to loss of resources which she could have drawn on. Thamilini also was not a good implementation architect and the excellent plans she undertook, she could not take them to their natural conclusion.

Thamilini reported to Tamilselvan during her role as the head of the women's division of the political wing. Some other women, but not Thamilini, criticized Tamilselvan for not giving full support to the work of women. Implementing plans to improve the women's lot still had to pass through Tamilselvan. Women accused him of changing the women in responsible positions. These women said that women working under a male must have the ability to challenge him. Yet, confronting him or any poruppalar runs the risk of being removed from the position. Thamilini's failure to take her plans to completion may have been due to her tendency to succumb to this pressure to conform.

The Two Males: Thileepan and Pirapaharan

Two important males who were behind the growth of the LTTE women must be mentioned here. Thileepan who was behind starting the SP did not live long enough to see it grow to its full potential on the social front. Many women who started their role as members of the SP expressed great respect and admiration for Thileepan's leadership style. They credited him for teaching the same to them. Some even said that they had never met another male like him in their lives.

Pirapaharan, on the other hand, urged the women to match the men in the military sector and succeeded. He sought the women's help to prove to the men, women's potential by making men and women compete and prove that women could do as well as the men. He managed to build confidence about the women among both the men and the women. Women commented that Pirapaharan was often aware of how men tried to sabotage the work of women in order to take the credit for themselves. Women said that he would take indirect actions to negate such sabotage. Women also claimed that when women and men stand in opposition, be it in describing an event or claiming credit or deciding who is telling the truth, Pirapaharan would always take the side of the women.

The style of struggle imagined by Thileepan and Pirapaharan appears different to the outsider. In reality they were not. What appears to be two different styles was in fact moulded by external historical changes and Thileepan's absence after the Indian intervention phase.

Geopolitics-6

During the ceasefire period, the peace talks were led by the European Union (EU). These have enabled the LTTE to gain some control of the Trincomalee harbour. Around this time, in 2003, USA launched its war on Iraq. USA considered the option of using the Trincomalee harbour during this war. The only other alternative the USA had was to use its single base in the Indian Ocean, the tiny Diego Garcia military base. It was known that the LTTE would not allow the Trincomalee harbour to be used as a military post by any external power. This was reason enough for the USA to destroy the EU lead peace process and to assist the Sri Lankan government in its genocidal war to destroy the LTTE.

One Permanent People's Tribunal document analyses the events during the period of the peace process and demonstrates how the USA went about undermining the peace process, first by holding an important donor meeting in the USA where the LTTE members were barred from participating because of the USA ban on the LTTE. The last straw for the peace process was the proscription of the LTTE by the European Union in 2006 under pressure from the USA and UK against the wishes of many EU member countries.

Another blow to the peace process came in the form of the 2004 tsunami. Though this too could have been a catalyst for strengthening the peace process, it was undermined by blocking tsunami funds reaching the people in the LTTE administered areas. Many more such actions by the UK-USA led establishment could be quoted which undermined the peace process and led to the all-out war from 2007 onwards.

The portrayal of the LTTE in the global mainstream media, prior to and during the peace process, must be seen in this geopolitical background. Thus, much of the mainstream writing about the LTTE or women members of the LTTE is a negative portrayal perpetuated by the above forces who clearly did not wish the struggle to succeed. Recent history is replete with similar stories of other armed struggles where the mainstream has negatively portrayed the legitimate struggles.

12
New Changes

This history document will skip the eighteen months period when the Eelam Tamil people living in the de facto state of Tamil Eelam was subjected to a genocidal attack destroying the entire de facto state structures. Recording this period was never the aim of this work which should really be a matter for international investigation. It has already been proclaimed as genocide by the Permanent People's Tribunal held in Bremen, Germany, in 2013.

If so, what can a history project say about the period after the genocide, which is ongoing according to the Tribunal verdict? It can describe how women were subjected to sexual assaults by the Sri Lankan military which continued after the war ended in May 2009. It can describe the brave struggle of the women to bring up their children single-handedly having lost their husbands in the war. But this work will not do that. There are several reports by Tamils and non-Tamils covering these topics. The international outfits never back away from writing reports about victims. That is their bread and butter.

This work is a documentation of the evolution of a 'new woman' in the de facto state of Tamil Eelam. It will conclude by reviewing what has happened to this 'new woman' in the post-2009 phase of history. In fact some outside writers, feeling brave in the post-2009 geopolitical atmosphere without the LTTE, have also cautiously ventured to write about this 'new woman'. This chapter will attempt to understand the loss of focus among the women for the Tamil Eelam struggle in this post-2009 phase. From the time the women were actively taking part in the armed struggle, in other words, the history till this time, evolved while Tamils worked towards parity of military power. Once this parity was destroyed the only power Tamils now have is the people power.

For decades if not centuries, Eelam Tamils have looked up to the idols and leaders of India and Tamil Nadu for inspiration. However, in the de-facto state, the women did not take up stories of brave military women in history from India or Tamil Nadu as their inspirational idols. The Eelam Tamil women were known to quote a story that took place more than one hundred years ago in their region. It is about a woman named Ariyaaththai. This story has been sung in long poetry form in the past. Ariyaaththai's story goes as follows.

In her village, Kumulamunai, in this de facto state, a rogue elephant was destroying people's property. All the males in the village, who were expert at taming elephants, tried to tame it but failed. One night Ariyaaththai went into the forest with a rope and came back early next morning riding that rogue elephant. The implication was that she tamed it using her intelligence. Yet, a few days later she was found dead and had been poisoned. She was killed for her success and for putting the males in the village to shame. The stories of the LTTE women, like Barathy and Malaimahal, will also be placed among the Eelam Tamil legendary stories as idols and inspirations for the future Tamil women. This, however, has not happened yet because of the geopolitical climate that is working to disperse the only power Eelam Tamils have, the people power. See Appendix A4 on Thamilini, who became a tragic victim of this geopolitical climate. In contrast to Thamilini's post-2009 story, there are lesser known post-2009 stories that throw light on the 'new woman' lying dormant.

Vettichelvi, a writer from the de facto state, continues to write in the hostile atmosphere but trying hard to stay truthful to the 'new woman'. One of her short stories ends as follows:

> 'What is it Muhuntha?', queried Aruna, her concerned friend. Yet, there was a happy smile on Aruna's face. The days when

> Aruna cried endlessly for her brother who had disappeared passed. She had just regained that smile on her face. Should this smile be wiped out again?
>
> Muhuntha just could not think of bringing lines of sorrow back on her friend's face. She played along. Throwing her arms open she demanded, 'Carry me to the well'. That was Muhuntha's attempt to hide her own state of mind.
>
> Aruna picked up her friend like a bundle and carried her to the well. Aruna's two little sisters who were sitting under a tree near the well burst out laughing seeing the antics of the two grown up friends.

It will be hard to find incidents real or fictional like the one above, where one young woman, has the strength and freedom to pick up another, except from the de facto state. Another real life example was played out in Kepapulavu, where the women launched a people's struggle to regain their land. At some stage in their struggle, they achieved partial victory. Protesting women carried their leader on their shoulders to celebrate their partial victory. Such a practice can take place only in the de facto state and nowhere else in the Tamil land. These are signs of a 'new woman', who evolved in the de facto state who could act freely in thought and action in the public space. Presently she is dormant after being pushed back into the private space for her physical safety.

What is described in the geopolitics box of this chapter are the various means by which the people's power of Eelam Tamils is dispersed and diverted. The diversionary tactics have succeeded in the short term. Eelam Tamils have tasted their Tamil Eelam State. Eelam Tamil women too have tasted a different way of being under that de facto Tamil Eelam state. Will they really give up all that buckling under the geopolitical manipulations?

Geopolitics-7

The pattern set in place during the colonial era continued during the ceasefire period and after. During the end of the war from 2007-2009, China too attempted to gain a hold on some of the strategic locations in the island. It provided heavy loans and arms for the war. The regime that carried out the 2009 genocide was thus aligned with China to the convenience of the UK-USA axis to complete the war.

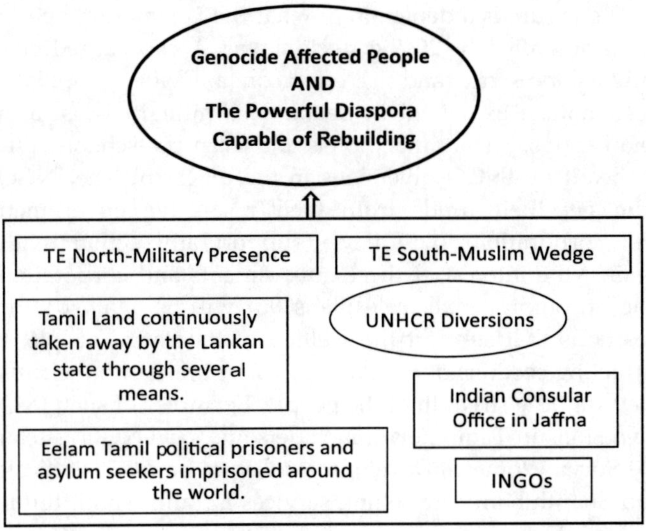

Immediately after the end of the war all the powers together blocked a discussion of this genocidal war at the UN Security Council. Instead the UK-USA axis was able to exploit the United Nations Human Rights Council (UNHCR) sessions to divert the energies and the resources of the Tamil Diaspora. These deceptions have continued for almost a decade, frustrating the Tamil diaspora. At the same time, the UNHCR deceptions were also used as campaign tools against the pro-China regime in Sri Lanka.

In 2015, the USA managed a regime change in Sri Lanka. The new regime was pro-USA. UNHCR sessions continued to pass resolutions, reports and warnings to keep the Tamil Diaspora's attention diverted.

In the homeland too, efforts on many fronts ensured that the Tamil people's attention remained diverted. These include: excessive military presence and related threats and destruction of community; a drama on a new constitution; continued imprisonment of Tamil people not only by the Sri Lankan regime but also around the world, INGO diversions, driving the wedge between Tamils and Muslims deeper.

The Figure is a depiction of what the Eelam Tamil people are facing after the 2009 genocidal war. A very large foreign military presence and its effect on a civilian population need not be explained in detail. This military runs farms, retail shops, restaurants, hotels and even pre-schools. What is meant by INGO diversions in the diagram? The INGOs, who get their funds from their respective governments and corporations, will never support any action that is against the interest of these governments and corporations. They promote small-scale plans but will be against strong positions that support the welfare of the entire people. By attracting sections of the affected community into their fold, they split the strength of the people. Examples of such INGO diversions in Tamil Eelam include some local NGOs such as the Surya Women's Development Centre based in Batticaloa and Shanthiham counselling services in Jaffna, both funded by USAID.

India is also providing new forms of diversion by opening a consular office in Jaffna. It invites artists from Tamil Nadu, who are against the Tamil nationalist sentiments that prevail even in Tamil Nadu. Instead, the artists, the consular office invites, ensure that Eelam Tamil sentiments on Eelam Tamil nationalism is diverted and erased. This consular office is also trying to introduce unknown cultural practices to the Eelam Tamils in order to blunt their nationalist sentiments.

The competition for real estate in the island continued to be fought by the four powers: USA, UK, India and China. People of the island are the losers.

A1: Book Excerpt

From page 156 of *Ilankaiyil Saathiyamum Athatku Ethiraana Pooraaddankalum* by Vehujanan and Raavana, 1989, South Vision, India. (Translation author)

In this manner, the upper caste could not tolerate the depressed classes coming forward to demand equal treatment in teashops. That night itself, the houses of the upper caste people, who supported the demand for equal treatment in the teashops were attacked. These communist comrades who supported the demand are, former head of Sanganai Town Council (Maan) and N. Muthaih. On the following days, the depressed classes in the Sanganai area were attacked with the help of the police. In particular, a village called Nichchaamam was targeted. On the August 17, 1967, guns were fired at them and their houses were burnt with the full support of the police. About fifty people were injured and many houses were burnt. In order to frighten those carrying out the attacks, the young men of Nichchaamam village set the loud crackers used in the fields. The fanatic upper caste attackers were forced to back away.

Chinnar Karthikesu (55) who was injured by the gun fire died. He became the first martyr in the revolutionary path begun on the 21st October revolution. Chinnar Karthikesu had participated in the Chunnakam uprising procession. With the same vigour he sacrificed his life. Many young men were arrested. Two young men sustained injuries due to sword cuts. The violence of the upper caste, assisted by the police, was on the increase. Arrests, beatings, torture, people forced to drink urine were all happening in the Sanganai police station. During this havoc by the police and the upper caste, one middle-aged woman had grabbed the gun from a policeman and told him, 'We will not back away out of fear for your gun'. It showed the determination of the people.

The revolution that began in 1967 in Sanganai continued till 1969. In the Sanganai police station there was Thamotharapillai, an upper caste fanatic. He was not only a fanatic but also an enemy of the communists. Therefore the police was firmly on the side of the upper caste. On the other side were the depressed people supported by the communist party.

The Sanganai people showed amazing bravery and skill in their protests against untouchability. They safeguarded themselves and broke the enemy's attacks using their collective experience. The caste fanatics gradually lost their vigour.

At the peak of the struggle, in February 1968, a young man Vanniyan Kumaresu, was killed by gun fire from the caste fanatics. The Nichchaamam people lost a second martyr in their struggle. His body was taken to the cemetery along the usual route. The caste fanatics attacked the funeral procession too. Thirty-two people were injured in this attack on the funeral procession. Three comrades who were leading the procession escaped by the breadth of a hair. Young men managed to stop the caste fanatics from going forward to continue their attack. The Sanganai police advised that the procession should proceed by a different route to escape attacks. The Nichchaamam people refused. They decided to take the body on the same route again. They made preparations to protect themselves. The police were forced to accept their decision and provide protection for them to take the body by the same route at 10 pm. A huge crowd took part in the funeral procession.

A2: Thamilini's Book

The people under the LTTE, from very different backgrounds socialized more as equals. The power distance and the manner of interaction were healthier. The societal structures and values put in place by the LTTE made this possible. After the destruction of these structures, the people carried over their earlier egalitarian relationships. However, very quickly the divide between those who have and those who have not widened. This gap started to exert itself strongly in the absence of the LTTE dominated societal structures and values. The haves, out of a sense of obligation, helped the have nots. This, however, is not a healthy state of affairs. Poverty and hardship of the have nots led to exploitation of the good will of the haves. The relationships between the two became one of benefactor-beneficiary with its associated deterioration. It is fair to say that in this regard, Thamilini was badly affected in the post-2009 atmosphere.

It is indeed impressive and tragic that finally she published a book post-2009. Many reviewers, writing in Tamil, about Thamilini's book, have challenged Thamilini's narrative, accusing her of lying or accusing others, connected with the release of her book posthumously, of altering the text. For a general reader, reading Thamilini's narrative, it is hard to sustain both these accusations. On the other hand, the reader would benefit by bearing in mind the following points.

Thamilini wrote her narrative living in Colombo, mainly under the Rajapakse regime, isolated from the Tamil people with whom she had lived and struggled until 2009. While

Thamilini notes the horrors visited on the Tamil, Muslim and Sinhala people by the LTTE, she probably mistakenly assumed that a discerning reader would already know the horrors visited and continuing to be visited on the Tamils by Sri Lanka and the world—before, during and after the civil war. Thamilini was in charge of the women's section of the political division of the LTTE since 1999. In her book she says:

> The role of the women's section of the political wing was to raise awareness in the society about women's rights, generally raise the position of women in the society, identify women left destitute and provide them with assistance, and generally work for broader positive changes in the society (translation by author).

Thamilini had left a void in her narrative about the work she did in this role. She does say that recruitment took most of her time. The five years of ceasefire from 2002 till recruitment began in earnest in 2006, was generally a period when a lot of development-related work was carried out in Vanni, socially, politically and economically. If there was nothing worthy of note that Thamilini implemented in these areas during this period, she has failed also to inform the reader the reasons for this.

Thamilini's narrative thus leaves the responsibility to the reader to situate it in a broader context.

A3: Tamil Eelam: De facto State Structure

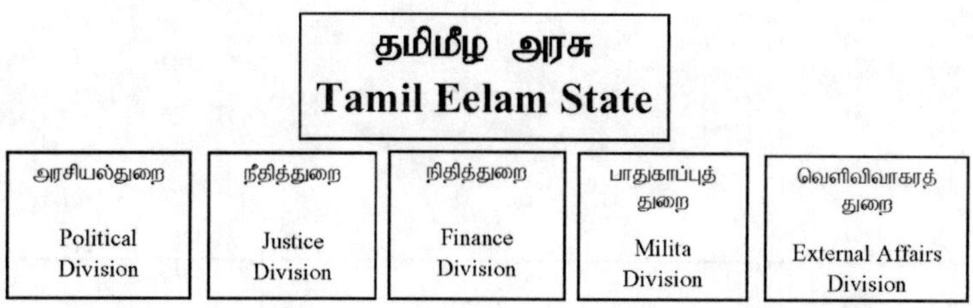

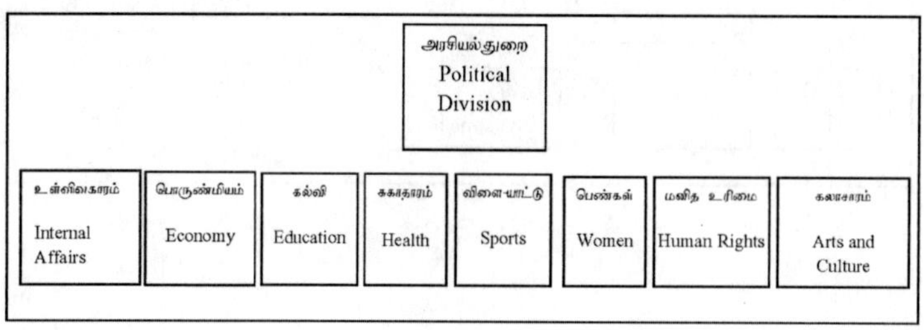

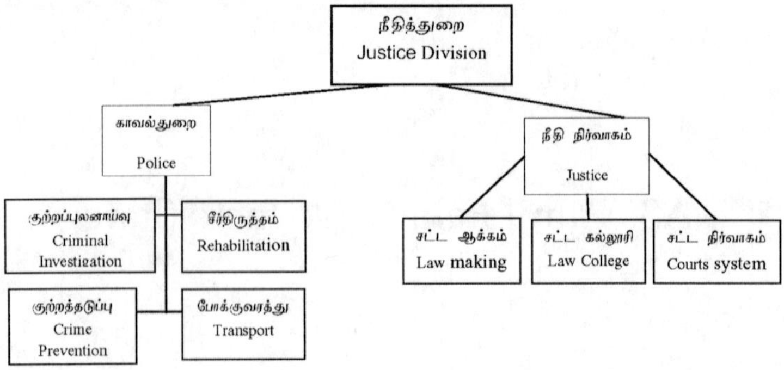
நீதித்துறை
Justice Division
காவல்துறை
Police
குற்றப்புலனாய்வு
Criminal Investigation
சீர்திருத்தம்
Rehabilitation
குற்றத்தடுப்பு
Crime Prevention
போக்குவரத்து
Transport
நீதி நிர்வாகம்
Justice
சட்ட ஆக்கம்
Law making
சட்ட கல்லூரி
Law College
சட்ட நிர்வாகம்
Courts system

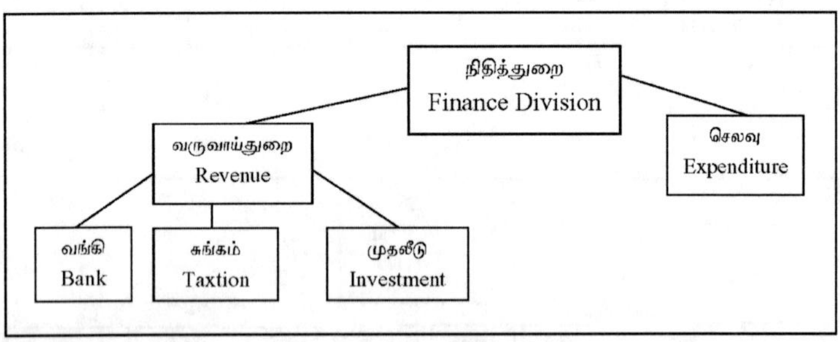
நிதித்துறை
Finance Division
வருவாய்துறை
Revenue
செலவு
Expenditure
வங்கி
Bank
சுங்கம்
Taxtion
முதலீடு
Investment

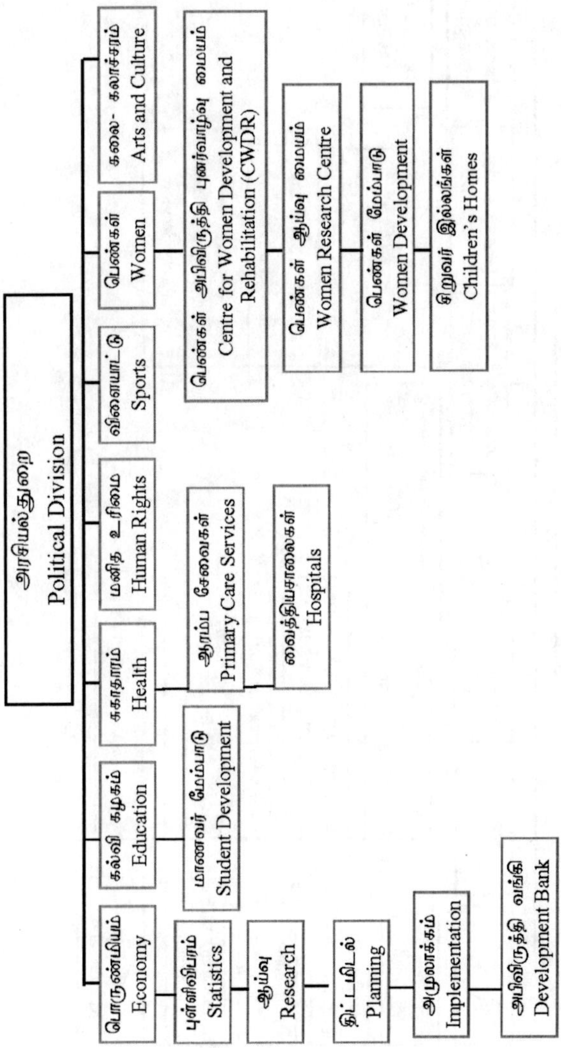
அரசியல்துறை
Political Division
பொருண்மியம்
Economy
புள்ளிவிபரம்
Statistics
ஆய்வு
Research
திட்டமிடல்
Planning
அமுலாக்கம்
Implementation
அபிவிருத்தி வங்கி
Development Bank
கல்விக் கழகம்
Education
மாணவர் மேம்பாடு
Student Development
சுகாதாரம்
Health
ஆரம்ப சேவைகள்
Primary Care Services
வைத்தியசாலைகள்
Hospitals
மனித உரிமை
Human Rights
விளையாட்டு
Sports
பெண்கள்
Women
பெண்கள் அபிவிருத்தி புனர்வாழ்வு மையம்
Centre for Women Development and Rehabilitation (CWDR)
பெண்கள் ஆய்வு மையம்
Women Research Centre
பெண்கள் மேம்பாடு
Women Development
சிறுவர் இல்லங்கள்
Children's Homes
கலை - கலாச்சாரம்
Arts and Culture

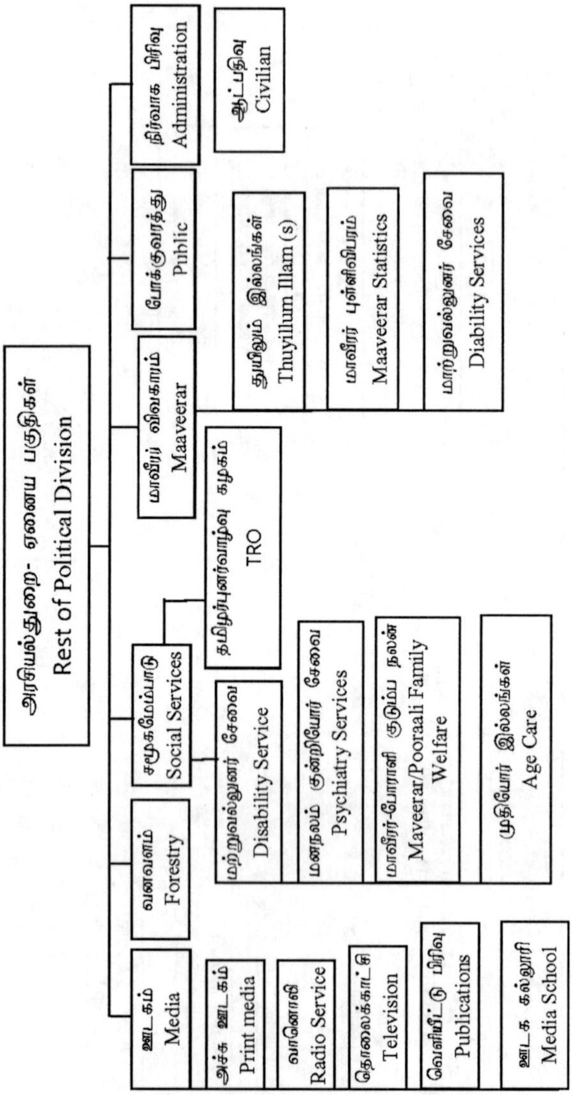
அரசியல்துறை- ஏனைய பகுதிகள்
Rest of Political Division
ஊடகம்
Media
அச்சு ஊடகம்
Print media
வானொலி
Radio Service
தொலைக்காட்சி
Television
வெளியீட்டு பிரிவு
Publications
ஊடக கல்லூரி
Media School
வனவளம்
Forestry
சமூகமேம்பாடு
Social Services
மாற்றுவலுவுளர் சேவை
Disability Service
மனநலம் குன்றியோர் சேவை
Psychiatry Services
மாவீரர்-போராளி குடும்ப நலன்
Maveerar/Pooraali Family Welfare
முதியோர் இல்லங்கள்
Age Care
தமிழர்புனர்வாழ்வு கழகம்
TRO
மாவீரர் விவகாரம்
Maaveerar
துயிலும் இல்லங்கள்
Thuyillum Illam (s)
மாவீரர் புள்ளிவிபரம்
Maaveerar Statistics
மாற்றுவலுவுளர் சேவை
Diability Services
போக்குவரத்து
Puhlic
நிர்வாக பிரிவு
Administration
ஆட்பதிவு
Civilian

Endnotes

1. *Women Fighters of Liberation Tigers*, Adele Balasingam, 1993. This book charts the growth of the battle capabilities of the women in the LTTE. The author Adele is an Australian who married Anton Balasingam, the LTTE theoretician. They lived among the LTTE for several years.
2. *Viluthaaki Veerumaaki*, The LTTE Malathi Regiment writers, 2005. This book in Tamil extends the above up to the latter period in more detail.
3. *A Fleeting Moment in My Country...*, N. Malathy, Clarity Press, USA, 2012 and Aakar Books, Delhi, 2013.
4. Bhakti refers to intense devotion to gods.
5. Pallava dynasty ruled the Tamil region of southern India during 7th century when Bhakti movement rose to its heights.
6. Cholas is one of the three dynasties that ruled different parts of the Tamil regions. Following the decline of Pallava dynasty, Cholas rose to great heights during 10th century.
7. Tamil Brahmi is the adoption of Emperor Asoka's Brahmi script for inscriptions in Tamil language.
8. Taraki Sivaram was a renowned Eelam Tamil journalist, who was murdered in 2004 by the paramilitary forces of the Sri Lankan Government.
9. International Human Rights Association based in Bremen, Germany (IMRV): http://humanrights.de
10. Permanent People Tribunal (PPT): http://www.ptsrilanka.org
11. *Ilankaiyil Saathiyamum Athatku Ethiraana Pooraaddankalum*, Vehujanan and Raavana, 1989, South Vision, India.
12. Ibid., p. 157
13. Ibid., p. 173
14. The rest of this chapter refers to several armed groups using their abbreviated names by which they are popularly known. The full expansion of these names are omitted for the sake of easier reading.
15. *Eela Pooraaddaththil Enathu Saadchiyam*, 2nd Edition, 2006, S. Pushparaja, Adaiyaalam.
16. A good example of the use of drama in the political struggle is 'Man Sumantha Meniyar' written by Kulanthai M Shanmugalingam which had been staged all over the homeland many times. This drama was later published by South Vision

and National Association for Art and Literature in 1998.

17. In Tamil 'pooraali' refers to someone who fights for justice. In the LTTE terminology it refers to its members.
18. In Tamil 'maaveerar' refers to a martyred great warrior. In LTTE terminology it refers to a member killed in battle.
19. At a later stage in the struggle, TRO (Tamil Rehabilitation Organization of the LTTE) took over the running of the preschool system and training the teachers and thus the pre-school movement continued till the end in 2009. During this phase the preschool movement gave young women employment. Though the remuneration given by TRO for the pre-school teachers was not high, young women, brought out in the public space through their participation in the preschool movement, gained greater awareness of events in the public space. However, the preschool movement run by TRO did not run as a social movement of the earlier times.
20. In Tamil 'poruppalar' refers to the one in charge of a unit/ organization of any size. It refers to the 'one who has the responsibility'.
21. The archive site http://www.noolaham.org has about 17 very old issues, including the very first issue of SP.
22. A female LTTE leader by the same name, Barathy, also appears in the following chapters of this book.
23. *Tamil Eelam* issue of January 1989, pp. 9-12, 'Un maranam emmil puthu moochchaai' by Vasanthi.
24. Shenuka's friend Ajanthi was killed the same year during a battle with the Indian forces. Shenuka left the movement soon after, less than a year after joining. Twenty years later, after the end of the civil war in 2009, while living in Australia, she published her "memoirs" of that time under the name *Niromi de Soyza*. The book is strewn, along with facts, inaccuracies and factual errors. Yet, this book was promoted by western activists and the western media because Shenuka's book reinforces the geopolitical campaign against the LTTE admirably.
25. *Viluthaaki Veerumaaki*: *History of Second Lt. Malathi Regiment*, by A. Kantha, S. Puradchikaa and Malaimahal, Second Lt. Malathi Regiment Publication, 2003.
26. Civil Administration in Tamil Eelam, Ethiveerasingam, http:// www.sangam.org/ ANALYSIS_ARCHIVES/civil.htm
27. This translation compilation is available as a PDF file at: www. wordpress.tamil tigerwomen.com.